DOGS

A Complete Guide to
More Than 200 Breeds

by Wendy Boorer
Illustrated by Doriene McQueen

Running Press
Philadelphia, Pennsylvania

First published in the United States of America in 1994 by
Running Press Book Publishers.

Text copyright © 1985, 1994 by Wendy Boorer
Illustration copyright © 1985, 1994 by Doriene McQueen

Originally published by HarperCollins Publishers Limited under the
title *Collins Gem Dogs*

9 8 7 6 5 4 3 2 1
Digit on the right indicates the number of this printing.

ISBN: 1-56138-382-1

Library of Congress Cataloging-in-Publication Number: 93-085521

Cover design by Toby Schmidt

Printed in Italy by Amadeus S.p.A.

This book may be ordered by mail from your publisher. Please
include $2.50 for postage and handling. *But try your bookstore first!*

Running Press Book Publishers
125 South Twenty-second Street
Philadelphia, Pennsylvania 19103-4399

Contents

Domestication and the Development of Breeds

Animals did not suddenly become domesticated at a particular time or place. Domestication must have been a continuing process, started and abandoned many times by early man. In the case of the dog, the earliest animal to be domesticated, this must have been even more true since it happened so long ago that success or failure to establish a working partnership must have remained local and isolated incidents. In some parts of the world primitive man was still trying to coerce, subdue, or otherwise manipulate primitive dog, while in other areas the development of an agricultural economy was already allowed man to take the first steps in selective breeding.

Scientists are generally agreed that an early form of the Asiatic wolf, *Canis lupus pallipes*, was the first canine to form a close association with humans. We do not know when this was, for the earliest evidence so far unearthed, which goes back to 12,000 B.C., suggest that it was already a dog that was co-existing with man and not a semi-tame wolf. The cooperation between the two species must have arisen through a common need which could be pursued to a common

Left: **Hunting played an important part in medieval life, manuscript illuminations like this one from a *Livre de Chasse* show hound being carefully looked after.**

benefit. Since these first contact occurred at a time in human development when people were hunters and gatherers of wild harvests, we must presume the common need was hunting, since both man and wolf were hunting the same prey. Both species would have the same technique, panicking the herds of herbivores, or isolating the old or the injured, the ones that were easier to kill. Humans had the advantage of hands to make and use weapons; wolves had the advantage of scent and speed. Both species lived in extended family groups, usually led by a dominant male animal. Both were nomadic over a wide area both were adaptable and also had the genetic flexibility which could produce wide variations of type within the same species. When a hunting party made a kill, or a wolf pack did the same, it was of interest to the other, since both were scavengers. As man improved his hunting skills the wolves would become more often the followers of man's hunting parties since these were more likely to produce pickings for all. Hanging around the campsites and the kills, the wolf packs would be able to provide an early warning of the presence of other predators. A certain tolerance would have grown up so that when the wolves, excited by the struggles of an injured animal, rushed in to finish it off, they would be regarded as useful partners rather than rivals. By encouraging a closer association man was already starting a select, for the best hunters would share the kill and the most tractable animals received their reward.

**Australia's wild dog:
the Dingo**

Somewhere during the long process of domestication, the wolf-like dogs would take the initiative of tracking and flushing game to be killed by man's superiors weaponry. Closer association enabled man to use these animals both for warmth and for food. By the time man tamed the reindeer, his second domestication species, the dog was far enough from its wild past to be used as a herding animal. It was also used for draft purposes, hauling the travois, a simple carrying device formed from two poles lashed together on which burdens could be rested. These dogs probably looked very like the smaller wolves, with the wedge-shaped head, prick ears, and bushy tail which was associate with the modern spitz breeds. Today's spitz are a non-specialist group among whom we can still find animals who perform all the tasks so far described.

With the establishment of settled farming communities in the Neolithic age, the domestication

Egyption mural

of goats, sheep, and cattle, and the cultivation of wheat and barley heralded a social revolution. The uses to which dogs could be put diversified. Domesticated animals needed guarding against predators. Crops needed protection against vermin. Hunting became a leisure pursuit rather than a necessity for survival. A settled existence meant that life was above the subsistence level and small house dogs were kept, valued for their watchfulness but also for their amusing ways.

Commodity surpluses led to the opening up of trade routes along which passed all the articles valued in the ancient world, including dogs. The fleetest, the fiercest, the smallest, and the best hunters all were valuable objects of barter. By the time the earliest surviving pictures of dogs were made on the walls of Egyptian tombs, there were already a number of widely different types, indicating that selective dog breeding must have been going on for some

thousands of years, by 2000 B.C. the Egyptians had, among others, elaborately spotted dogs, short-legged low to the ground dogs, dogs with erect ears and tightly curled tails, and drop-eared greyhounds. Dogs were held in great veneration over much of Egypt, and the Egyptians were among the most skilled of animals breeders, keeping a semi-domestication many animals which are regarded today as wild. The greyhound, the dog which hunts by sight, and overtakes its quarry by sheer speed, originated in this area, where the hot, dry desert air gave good visibility but poor scenting conditions. Further to the east, large mastiffs hunted lion, fought in the battles beside their masters, and were famed for their courage throughout the Mediterranean civilisations. The Greeks kept and developed a number of hound breeds. They needed dogs who would track quarry through cooler, more humid woodland. They also used a sheep and herding dogs and appreciated toy dogs as companion animals.

It was not only as trade goods, in exchange for amber, tin, silks, and spices that dogs traversed the ancient world. Throughout history invading armies have taken dogs with them, or brought them back from their area of conquest.

The medieval passion for hunting led to the development of more varieties of hunting dog, each noble vying with the next to produce a superior strain. The development of the gun was paralleled by the development of specialist breeds of dog to find and bring back the game. In the twentieth century man is still altering the dog, though the biggest influence today is show ring fashion. There are types of dog being selected for their ability rather than their appearance even today, such as police and service dogs, and working sheepdogs, but most modern purebred animals are bred for their looks, their function being that of companions rather than workers.

Dachshunds and terriers retain the urge to dig and to explore a burrow even when mainly kept as pets.

The Natural History of the Dog

The concept of pure-breeding, having ancestors all of the same type, and the idea of keeping a pedigree recording all those ancestors, have much more importance now than in the past. Dog showing, which started in England in 1859, is a sport which very rapidly spread worldwide. It soon became evident that some controlling body would have to devise and enforce rules for such competitions and, in 1873, the English Kennel Club was founded. Now nearly every country in the world has its own Kennel Club.

A Kennel Club's functions include the registration and the recording of all pedigree stock and the licensing and control of all dog shows, field trials, working trials, and obedience competitions. They also register and license breed clubs, canine societies, and dog training societies. In some countries they license judges. Kennel Clubs issue breed standards, written descriptions of ideal animals. It is with these ideals in mind that a judge makes his or her awards in the show ring. The standards tend to vary from country to country. Size and permissible colors may differ slightly but the most marked difference in show dogs round the world is whether or not their ears are cropped. Cropping involves cutting off the ear flaps to leave a point. This is a painful operation, performed under a general anaesthetic when the dog is about three months old. The operation serves no useful purpose and has been banned in Britain for almost 100 years. Some breeds are customarily cropped in America and Europe, though the European Community plans soon to ban all such fashionable mutilations. Docking (cutting off all or part of the tail of a newborn puppy), is an even more widespread practice, again rarely justifiable. The size and weight quoted throughout this book are approximately those for an adult male. Females are usually slightly smaller and lighter.

Through domestication and selective breeding by man, the dog now displays the widest divergence of type known within a single species of animal. This is possibly most noticeable in respect of weight, the largest breeds weighing 60 plus times that of the smallest. Other effects of domestication include changes in the digestive tract, loss of full dentition in many breeds, and the retention of juvenile characteristics, particularly with regard to temperament. Underneath the skin all dogs have the same bone structure, except for the bones of the tail, for there are one or two breeds that are tailless. Another variable is the presence of otherwise of dew-claws, found on the inner side of the lower leg. These are often on the front leg and some breed standards specify their removal. Occasionally they appear on the hindlegs, where they are nearly always removed by the breeder, except in the two breeds where double hind dew-claws are a breed characteristic.

The dog is a successful species because of its

adaptability and this applies to its nutrition among other things. Research carried out by dog food manufacturers has established the essential requirements of a canine diet in some detail, but the dog can, and does, obtain these basic nutrients from a wide variety of sources. Adult dogs can thrive on a maintenance diet of comparatively low protein (18% dry matter basis), but breeding animals or growing animals should have this level raised to 25%. Cereal products require cooking before a dog can digest them and fat is essential. A diet consisting solely of lean meat and biscuit would not be adequate. Vitamins and minerals are as necessary for the dog as for man, with the exception of vitamin C, which the dog is able to synthesize. It is quite natural for a dog to bolt chunks of food, for its saliva does not assist in digestion but merely acts as a lubricant.

Sexual maturity is achieved by different breeds at different ages, but on average males become fully fertile around ten months. Ovulation occurs in the bitch during a oestrus period known as being in season or "in heat". On average a bitch will come into season twice a year for a period of three weeks each time, but there are many variations on this pattern. Though attractive to males earlier, a bitch will not accept a mate until somewhere about the 11th to the 14 day after first showing a discharge from her vulva. During this receptive period, if she is allowed to do so, a bitch will accept a number of males and can have a litter sired by different fathers. The mating may or may not be accompanied by a "tie", during which the dogs are physically locked together so tightly that the two animals cannot be parted. On average a tie lasts about ten minutes. It occurs only in the dog, wolf, and fox. Its significance is unknown – it is not necessary for conception. The gestation period for a bitch to produce a viable litter is 63 days (plus or minus nine).

Most bitches prefer to whelp (give birth) in a small, dark, enclosed space. One reason is that the puppies are born without any functioning means of temperature regulation and depend for warmth on keeping close to their mother in a space small enough to be heated by her own body heat. Whelping time is indicated by restlessness and a drop in the bitch's temperature. Once contractions have started the first puppy should be born within two hours. After removing the puppy from the membranes surrounding it the bitch will dry and stimulate it by licking and eat the afterbirth.

Newborn puppies of whatever breed look much the same shape, with blunt muzzles, tightly closed eyes, and folded ears. Although blind and deaf, puppies move toward warmth and have a sense of smell which enables them to locate the bitch's teats. Very young, healthy puppies do little but feed and sleep. At this stage the pup's tongue seems disproportionately large, almost a wrap-round device for increasing the suction on a nipple. The struggle for supremacy is evident from the start, with the strongest puppies

Top: **Hand-rearing is difficult and time consuming.**
Bottom: **Dachshund bitch with litter of puppies.**

tucking themselves into the warmest position with the best milk supply under their mother's thigh.

The puppies' eyes open from ten days onward and hearing begins to function at about the same time. By three weeks of age the puppies are walking instead of crawling, playing with their littermates, and reacting to outside influences. They are also starting to eat solid foods, weaning being a gradual process that should be complete by seven weeks. In the wild the puppies would be weaned by the adults regurgitating partially digested food and some bitches will do this even in domestic situation. Litter size varies with breed size. Giant dogs may have 12 or more in a litter. Toy breeds only two. Breed size also has an influence on longevity. Giant breeds are old at seven. Breeds such as the small terriers start ageing at about 11 years. It is exceptional, but not unknown for a dog to live to 20 plus years.

Puppies need the constant companionship of their littermates up to the age of seven weeks. Their playing and mock fighting enable them to establish on order of dominance, an experience which enables them, when adult, to react normally to their own species. Their mother's discipline is also important from seven to twelve weeks old they need to gain confidence by experiencing various outside influences. Being handled by a number of different people, being introduced to different places, getting accustomed to different noises – all are necessary if the puppy is to become a bold and self-confident adult. Puppies that by 12 weeks have never seen a human, remain irredeemably wild, a fact that throws an interesting side-light on the process of domestication.

The dog is a social animal, a pack having an hierarchy whereby the weaker members defer to the stronger. This type of behavior if the foundation on which the successful man/dog relationship is built. By training, man reinforces his position as pack leader.

Dogs are territorial, marking their ownership by urination. Previously house-broken dogs will often mark every room in a new house before reverting to clean habits. This scent-marking plays a very important role in commun-ication. A dog spies out the land by using its nose rather than its eyes. Sight is a less important sense to the dog than either scent or sound. The flicker of movement will draw a dog's attention but a stationary object too far away to be scented will be unnoticed. Visual commun-ication between dogs is by means of facial expression, body posture, and tail carriage.

17

Hound Breeds

Bassets are among the short-legged hunting hounds, part of a group of dogs distinguished not only by their lowness to the ground, but also by their excellent scenting powers. All the Basset breeds originated in France, a country where the hunting tradition is so strong that there are a large number of breeds of pack hounds.

The **Basset Hound**, a smooth-coated, very heavily boned dog on short, crooked legs, is the most familiar of these dogs in America and Britain. The average Basset weighs about 55lb, so, though the height may be under 15in, this is by no means a small dog. The heavily wrinkled skin and the pendulous ears, which should reach at least to the end of the muzzle, give

Basset Griffon Vendéen

the dog a doleful expression which is misleading, since they are heartly, rollicking dogs with big appetites for food and exercise. Having a history of communal living (packs average about 15 couple of hounds – 30 dogs) Bassets do not take kindly to a solitary existence and can be noisy in protest. As befits a dog bred to puzzle out a cold trail, they are persistent and obstinate.

The **Basset Griffon Vendéen** has a harsh, shaggy coat which is a more lightly built, less exaggerated, low to ground dog. It is used in France for hunting most small game, either in packs or working alone. The dog's kindly expression, tousled appearance, and gently waving tail are all very appealing.

The **Basset Fauve de Bretagne** is just beginning to be shown in Britain. The wire coat is always wheaten or a golden fawn in color.

Basset Hound

The **Beagle**, the smallest of the British scent hounds, was almost entirely kept as a working dog until the 1940s, when it began its climb to popularity as a companion and a show dog. The name can be traced back to the 15th century, when diminutive fox-beagles were kept: some were very tiny, under 10in, and could be carried on horseback. The hare, which is now the proper prey for a beagle pack, only came to be regarded as such in the late 18th century. Beagling is a sport which is carried out on foot. For the followers it resembles a cross country run, with the added delights of watching hounds puzzling out a line and listening to the hound music as they give tongue on a scent. There are still plenty of beagle packs in existence, some of which can trace their hounds' breeding back over 150 years.

The Beagle has become an extremely popular pet on both sides of the Atlantic. It is an active, strong

Beagle

Basenji

dog and, being about 16in in height, a very convenient size to fit into most modern homes. The tip of the tail should be white but the smooth coat can be any recognized hound color – which means black, tan, and white, or any mingling of these three, which are the colors expected in Bassets, Fox-hounds, Harriers, and Beagles. Many Beagles are tri-colors with a black saddle over the back, the richness of the coloring adding to their smart appearance. They are merry dogs, active and outgoing, albeit with the obstinacy and willfulness that besets all the scent hounds when an enticing odor wafts across their path.

The **Bassenji** is one of the more unusual hunting dogs of the world and one that has had a long history, for gracefully built dogs with erect ears and the very characteristic, tightly curled, ring tail appear first in the murals in ancient Egyptian tombs. Victorian explorers in Africa came across and commented upon similar dogs, especially in the Congo basin. There they were used by their native owners to find and drive game into nets. They had a number of distinguishing features among which was their inability to bark. Because of this they often wore wooden bells to help the tribesmen locate them when working their way through the elephant grass, which completely hid the dogs from view.

A few dogs from the Sudan were taken to Britain in the 1930s. African owners of hunting dogs would not readily part with quality stock but by the late 1940s the breed was established both in Britain and America. The coat is sleek and fine, either bright red, glossy black, or black and tan, all set off by white markings. The skin is supple and pliant, with the forehead being covered with fine, profuse wrinkles giving the dog an expression of quizzical scrutiny. Its fine bones accentuate the gazelle-like grace of the animal. Ideal size is 17in with a weight about 24lb. Basenjis can be quarrelsome with other dogs, nor are they really mute, making a wide variety of yodels, yelps, and yells when sufficiently provoked. They are exceptionally clean dogs, using their paws to wash, rather like cats.

The **Black and Tan Coonhound** is, as the name suggests, a specialist in hunting the racoon and the opossum. This is a tough and demanding sport, and a number of coonhound breeds have been developed, though the Black and Tan is the only one

Bloodhound **Black and Tan Coonhound**

recognized as a show dog as well as a worker. Coon hunting takes place at night during the autumn and winter months. The hounds trail this nocturnal animal and their owners follow the hound's progress by the melodious baying for which all the coonhound breeds are noted. Many licensed hunting trials take place every year, with marks being given for the dog's performance when following a scent and in finally treeing the racoon. The Black and Tan is a very powerful and agile hound, standing about 27in at the shoulder.

The **Bloodhound** is the largest of the hounds that hunt by scent, with males weighing up to 110lb and measuring 27in. Bloodhounds are famous for their tenacity in puzzling out a cold line and are believed to have the most sensitive noses of any breed of dog. Certainly some remarkable tracking feats have been recorded by police using bloodhound, the dogs becoming so totally absorbed in their task that they are oblivious to any outside distraction. Oddly enough, the killing instinct seems almost totally lacking in the purebred Bloodhound which, when it finds its man at the end of the trail, is more likely to bowl him over with joyful exuberance than knock him down with harmful intent.

St. Hubert's Abbey, founded in the Ardennes in A.D., 687, was famed for the quality of its hounds, and it is from the black St. Hubert's hound that the Bloodhound descends. The modern dogs can be black and tan, red and tan, or red in color. The Bloodhounds' most extraordinary characteristic is the amount of loose skin about its head and neck. This skin, which is thin and supple, hangs in deep folds and wrinkles, particularly when the dog has its nose down. The hanging flews (upper lips), the pendulous dewlaps, and the long soft ears all combine to give the dog an expression of dignity and solemnity. It comes as rather a shock to find that many Bloodhounds are reserved and rather sensitive dogs by nature. Their size and heavy bone make them look rather clumsy until they break into the elastic, swinging, ground-covering stride which is so characteristic of the breed.

The **Dachshund** has a distinctive shape which lends itself to caricature and cartoon. There are other dogs as long and as low as the Dachshund, but none have achieved the same renown with the general public. A German breed, it was expected to follow a scent and pursue its prey (usually a badger) underground, hold it at bay in its earth and bark continuously to indicate their position to the men above waiting to dig the badger out. Dachshunds are therefore shaped to go down holes, have strong jaws to defend themselves, short legs and big feet for efficient digging, and a big rib cage to add resonance to the noise that the dog is expected to make. The bark of a Dachshund has the timbre of that from a much bigger dog.

**Smooth
Dachshund**

Long-haired Dachshund

Wire-haired Dachshund

Queen Victoria's Germanic husband introduced the Dachshund to Britain. In the 19th century the dogs look far more hound-like, standing higher on the ground with the legs more crooked. Today six breeds of Dachshund are recognized, divided by coat and by size. there is a standard and a miniature variety in the Smooth-haired, the Long-haired, and the Wire-haired Dachshund. The ideal structure is the same for each breed, and the colors include red, black and tan, chocolate, and dapple, in practice the **Smooth-haired Dachshund** appears the longest of the three coated varieties and, given the opportunity, manages to combine a strong interest in hunting with a sybaritic passion for comfort and food. The **Long-haired**

Dachshund seems the most elegant, with the slight suggestion of a roman nose and shining falls of wavy hair. The Wire-haired Dachshund is very much the country gentleman, strong-willed with a quizzical expression given by beetling eyebrow and bushy whiskers.

The **Scottish Deerhound** should not be less than 30in high and should weight 103lb though it should be noted that this is one of the breeds in which bitches are noticeably smaller. This means that the Deerhound is about half the size and weight of the red deer of the Scottish Highlands, which the dog was bred to course. Deer coursing, where pairs of dogs were slipped to chase and pull down a stag or hind, was the sport of highland clan chieftains. The Highland clearances of the 18th century destroyed the

Scottish Deerhound

27

clan structure, the development of the sporting rifle diminished the need for a coursing dog, and Deerhound numbers declined. However, these gentle aristocrats have an appeal which ensure their survival and today more interest is taken in them than at any time in their long history. The Deerhound coat is harsh and wiry, with dark blue-gray being the preferred color.

The **English Foxhound** is a working animal, bred and maintained solely for the purpose of fox hunting. Hound packs may differ in the types they prefer differences that may be dictated by the terrain or, in the case of color, by tradition. However, these are superficial points when compared with Foxhound essentials: stamina, speed, scenting ability, and giving tongue when hunting a line. The 18th century saw the decline of stag hunting and the rise in fox hunting. A number of packs can trace the breeding of their hounds back this far, making foxhounds the oldest of recorded pedigree animals. Changes in agriculture meant faster horses and faster hounds could be used, the problem always being not to sacrifice strength and stamina for speed. Following a line of scent is made ever more difficult today by pollution, chemical fertilizers, and the internal combustion engine. Foxhounds have been one of England's most successful exports, since emigrating aristocrats often took packs of hounds with them. These contributed to the foundation stock of a number of other hunting breeds in different parts of the world.

English Foxhounds

The **Hamiltonstovare** is a Swedish hound named after the breed's creator, a gentleman who wanted a handsome dog of proven working ability. The Hamiltonstovare is a general purpose hunting dog used for tracking on its own, rather than working as a pack animal. Swedish hunting conditions ensure that the breed is a hardy one, but the dog's appearance and affectionate nature have also ensured popularity as a show dog and companion. The height should be about 22in and the striking tri-coloration is a breed characteristic.

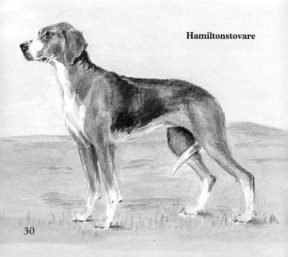

Hamiltonstovare

Segugio

The **Segugio** is the only native Italian scent hound. Though widely used and popular for hare hunting, few Segugio today are purebred so a revival of interest is needed in the pedigree animal. The Segugio is a quiet and gentle dog with an elegant outline which suggest speed as well as stamina. The coat can either be smooth or wire-haired and should be either red, or black and tan. The head is long and rather narrow with lustrous, almond-shaped eyes described as dark ochre in color. Seen in profile the muzzle is very slightly convex and this, together with the long, drooping ear, suggests a common ancestry with some of the French hound breeds. Height can be up to 23in. The Segugio is not usually used as a pack hound, being more often worked singly or in a couple. Its prey is mostly hare, which the dogs are expected to find, track, and drive toward the hunter.

31

The **Ibizan Hound** is one of a number of hunting dogs of the greyhound family, found at the western end of the Mediterranean. As the name suggests, they are found on the island of Ibiza, one of the Balearic group, but also on the Spanish mainland. They are tall, narrow, finely built dogs with erect ears which are long and very mobile. The coat can be either smooth or rough but it always close and dense. The color is very often white with chestnut or lion (sandy) patches. The nose is a pinkish brown colored and the eyes are amber, which gives a rather staring expression. Ibizan Hounds are used for rabbit catching, either singly, or in small packs.

The **Pdengo** is a very similar type of dog to the Ibizan Hound, especially in the largest of its three sizes, but found further west, in Portugal. It is also a hare and rabbit hunting dog, the smallest Podengo being expected to enter warren to bolt the rabbits into waiting nets.

Pharaoh Hound

The **Pharaoh Hound** is found on the island of Malta and is another alert, keen hunter using both eyesight

Ibizan Hound

and scent to follow its prey. It is rather smaller than the Ibizan – 22in as opposed to 27½in, is smooth-coated and glossy, and should be a bright tan all over with white markings in the extremities. On Malta the breed is called *Kelb Tal-Kenek* and was only dubbed Pharaoh Hound when it reached the British show scene. This breed resembles one of the ancient Egyptian hunting dogs, and also their dog-headed deity, anubis, and this is why the name Pharaoh Hound was chosen.

All these breeds are very keen hunters, will retrieve to hand, and are excellent jumpers.

33

The **Rhodesian Ridgeback** is a muscular, heavy set rather plain-looking dog with a height of 27in and a weight around 80lb. Its muzzle is often dark, giving a surly and suspicious look to what is a first–class guard and a courageous hunting animal. The breed is the national one of South Africa. Early ancestry was mixed, the most important ingredient being a type of dog belonging to the original inhabitant of South Africa, the Hottentots. These were pastoralists whose dogs were expected to guard the flocks and herds from two-legges as well as four-legged predators. Since the Cape of Good Hope at that time teamed with big game, such dogs were also used for hunting. They resembled today's breed in only three particulars: they were reddish tan in color, they were courageous without being foolhardy, and they had a curious ridge of hair running down the spine, lying the opposite way to the rest of the coat. The peculiarity survived a lot of cross breeding, for European settlers brought their hounds and gundogs with the. Many of their dogs were not robust enough to withstand the climate or the parasites and diseases of their new homeland, so the tough little native dog was crossed in to make various imported hunting dogs hardier. In the process it gained increased size and a very good nose. Early Ridge-backs guarded lonely farms and hunted big game for the European settlers. They got the nickname "lionhound" because they would track lion quite silently, bark when they had the animal at bay and dodge snap, feint, and back off, holding the lion's attention until someone could shoot it. The breed was a very rough and ready one until 1922, when an official standard was drawn up by interested South African and Rhodesian breeders. The breed today hunts wild pig, cougar, lynx, and crop-raiding baboon in various parts of the world. They are also loyal and dignified guards, devoted to their owners and naturally suspicious of strangers.

Rhodesian Ridgeback

Otterhounds

Otterhounds provide an interesting example of what can happen to a breed when the original purpose for which it was bred no longer exists. In a last ditch conservation effort, the hunting of the otter was banned in Britain, and the two remaining packs of purebred Otterhounds then also needed conservation. These large packhounds with rugged constitutions show great persistence when hunting since the scent of an aquatic animal such as the otter is one of the most difficult trials to follow. Their dedication to following elusive scents makes them deaf to all command when unravelling a line, so they are not suitable dogs for the average pet owner. Some Otterhounds were resettled with exhibitors who had kennelling and enthusiasm to provide the facilities for exercise needed by so large and active a dog. Other attempts are being made to retrain the hounds to hunt feral mink.

Otterhounds are large dogs 27in high and weighing 90lb, the males are often considerably larger than the females. The coat is double with a thick woolly undercoat under the coarse outer hair. The dog smells very pungent when wet but the protective hair allows the Otterhound to swim and wade in freezing water without harm. The coat is either gray or sandy or a mixture of the two the colors soft and muted in shade as if constant immersion in water has faded them.

The **Afghan Hound** is noted for its regal bearing. It is another member of the greyhound family, which originated in the countries bordering the eastern Mediterranean. Spread along the trade routes of the ancient world, such sighthounds reached Afghanistan, where their worth in hunting gazelle and fox was fully appreciated. Many centruies later these long-coated running dogs were seen and admired by British army officers doing a tour of duty in northern India. Occasionally they were able to acquire one and so a few of these exotic-looking creatures began to arrive in Britain where they created enough interest for a breed club to be formed in the 1920s.

Afghanistan itself had at least two types of hound but these have now been blended together to form one breed. Its admirers find the aloof and dignified stare an irresistible attraction. The long, finely textured hair gives a bizarre distinction to the dog's appearance, and the springy, stylish gait is very eye-catching. These are dogs built to travel at top speed over very rough terrain, which requires power, stamina, and strong motivation. New owners, attracted by the dogs' fashionable appeal, have not always appreciated that they are getting a dog whose hunting instinct far outstrips its desire to please its owner. The coat, too, is deceptive. Magnificent when properly groomed, the long fine texture means that it mats very easily if neglected. Male can be 29in in height and all colors are acceptable in the show ring.

Afghan

The **Borzoi** was known until fairly recently as the Russian Wolfhound, for it was a dog kept in Imperial Russia for coursing wolves, a ceremonial kind of hunting and a fashionable country pursuit for the sporting nobility. The Borzoi is a strongly built sighthound with a thick, silky coat. The breed was developed from the Persian greyhound in the 17th century. The latter proved too delicate for the

Russian winter so it was crossed with native sheepdogs to improve coat and stamina. Rivalry between landowners with kennels of hounds kept in extravagant numbers refind the breed to the strong, speedy, elegant animal we know today. Queen Victoria was presented with some by the Tsar of Russia and it became fashionable to own one. The Borzoi has an exceptionally long and lean head with a dark eye and strong jaws. The body is a series of graceful, flowing curves, giving an impression of streamlined strength. The color is often white with patches of red or black. The minimum height is 29in, so this is a big dog with plenty of stylish grace.

Borzois

Greyhound

Greyhounds have a particularly long recorded history. Streamlined and fast, the greyhound types appeared first in the middle East where a keen-sighted dog was needed to course gazelle and desert fox. They were valued animals, and their progress is recorded in the murals of 3000 B.C. in Egypt, in the decorations on Greek and Roman pottery, and in the lists of gifts from one medieval European ruler to another, when greyhounds were considered to have enough merit to honor a king. It is possible that the breed reached England about 400 B.C. when Phoenician traders landed in Cornwall to barter for

41

tin. Early legislation confined the ownership of greyhounds to those of rank who could be expected to own the land on which such dogs would hunt. In the 18th century, coursing became a formalized sport where two dogs are loosed together after a hare and judged on their speed and skill in the chase. Greyhound racing started to become popular in America in the early part of the century, and the first track was opened in England in 1926. Both coursing and racing are betting sports, and the latter has had the result that more and faster greyhounds are being bred all the time. Though sheltering under the same breed name, there is a subtle difference between coursing and racing dogs. The show ring greyhound is a different type again. The exhibitor's dog is larger in size, more exaggerated in outline, and with a particularly fine, close coat. Show dogs can be as tall as 30in at the shoulder, and can be almost any color. Greyhounds are gentle and affectionate toward their owners but the instinct to chase and kill any small

Sloughi

running creature makes owning them a worrying responsibility.

The **Sloughi** is one of the rarest of the sighthounds. It originated in Morocco as an offshoot of the greyhound group, spreading west along the coast of North Africa. It is a smooth-coated, lean, muscular dog, affectionate toward its owner and indifferent to the rest of the world. The main differences to be noticed in this breed are in the head, which is stronger and flatter than in other sighthound breeds.

Greyhound racing

43

The **Irish wolfhound** is the largest breed in the world, the minimum height for dogs being 31in and the minimum weight 20lb. So majestic an animal is described by the Irish as "similar in shape to a Greyhound, bigger than a Mastiff, and as tractable as a Spaniel". References to Celtic hounds abound in Greek and Roman writings, where frequent mention is made of their size and courage. The heroes and chieftains of early Irish history had such hounds and, when the Danes started raiding Irish shores in the 7th century, they too were astonished at the stature of these dogs. However, tribal warfare and wolves both declined in Ireland and by the early 1800s the Irish Wolfhound was almost extinct. It was left to an Englishman, Captain Graham, to resuscitate the breed and publicize them enough to ensure their survival.

The Wolfhound's great height is accompanied by an air of commanding strength and an impressive bulk. The coat is rough and wiry, usually either gray or wheaton, though a number of other colors are acceptable. The eye is dark and gentle in expression, Wolfhounds being an exceptionally docile and manageable breed for their size. As with all the giant breeds, rearing plays a very big part and requires a certain skill. Such big dogs take a long time to reach maturity, often not finishing their growth until they are three years old or more. To achieve their full potential size and weight these very big breeds all need adequate food, controlled exercise, and plenty of rest.

Irish Wolfhound

The **Saluki** is believed to be oldest purebred type of the sighthound family and its nickname, Gazelle Hound, indicates its original function. The Bedouin treasured the Saluki, breeding it with as much care as their Arab horses. These hunting dogs shared the tents of their nomadic masters, their genealogy being handed down as part of the oral tradition of the tribe.

The Saluki is lithe, graceful, and swift, with a proudly-held head carriage. The term far-seeing is used of the Saluki's expression, and this is not a figurative use of the term for these dogs will watch birds far in the distance, a legacy of their desert past when they were used for hawking. Their reactions are so fast that Salukis have been known to catch partridge as they rise from the ground in front of the dog. The coat is smooth and silky with feathering in the legs and tail. Height up to 28in.

Saluki

Lurchers

The **Lurcher** is a working type, not a pedigree breed, but it exists in some number, owned by people who admire and use its speed and skill. They always have greyhound or whippet on one side of the family. The other side is often a working sheepdog, which adds patience, brains, and a desire to please to the mixture. The resultant animals are a very mixed bunch, often with broken or rough coats. Similar dogs with speed, silence, and cunning to catch enough to feed both themselves and their masters are found in many countries.

47

The **Whippet** was originally produced in the north of England in the first half of the 19th century to satisfy the sporting tastes of miners. Rabbit coursing in an enclosed space, with the kills timed against a stopwatch, was the local betting sport. Terriers, the forefathers of such breeds as the Manchester and the Bedlington, were not really fast enough, so judicious crossing took place with small greyhounds.

When rabbit coursing was made illegal because of the cruelty involved, the miners turned to racing their dogs, training them to run and grip and worry a rag shaken by their owners. Rag racing called for improved quality in the dogs, who became more streamlined and considerably faster. Handlers would hold the dog on the starting line and literally throw it up the track when the gun was fired. Various systems

Whippet

Whippet

of handicapping were tried and whippet racing got a bad name for chicanery. Greyhound racing, with its lavish commercial backing, finally finished the backyard rag racing. By this time the Whippet had become known in the show ring and had spread to Europe and the United States. In the 1950s Whippet racing was revived as an amateur sport. Starting traps in miniature, similar to those used in greyhound racing, are used and there is no betting, the meetings being run for the fun of the participants. There is no division of types as there is in the greyhound. The same Whippet can win in the show ring one day and win on the track the next. Whippets should be about 18½in in height, but many are larger than the ideal. The short smooth coat can be any color or mixture of colors. The look of fragility belies their inherent toughness.

49

Spitz Breeds

Spitz are often considered northern dogs, perhaps because huskies are so widely recognized, but they are spread world-wide and there is no evidence to suggest that they spread out from the center, as the greyhounds did. The existence of so many indigenous spitz breeds suggest that these are possibly the oldest type of domesticated dog.

The **Elkhound**, a very typical member of the spitz group of breeds, is classified among the hounds in Britain because it hunts by scent. The breed is Norwegian and the density of the coat alone would suggest that it was bred for work in a cold climate. It is a bold dog, independent in spirit and workmanlike in appearance. In Norway it is used both as a sorting companion and as a guard and general purpose farm dog. These dogs have been used to hunt reindeer and bear but, as the name suggest, their principal quarry is the elk (known to Americans as the moose). Elkhounds usually track singly, either running ahead loose from the start or being released from the leash when the moose is sighted. The dog must force the moose to stand at bay, which it does by dancing in and out, barking furiously, and dodging the retaliation of hoof and horn. The dog may have to hold the moose in the same place for anything up to an hour before it can be dispatched, so there is plenty of power and stamina in the sturdy frame. Its four-square appearance helps the dog bounce and dodge in and out. The initiative has to remain with the Elkhound, which is why the

Elkhound

breed are often characters with minds of their own. Like many other northern dogs the Elkhound has a double coat and is extremely dense. It is always various shades of gray with black tips on the end of the guard hairs. The height is about 20½in and the weight 50lb. A few Elkhounds are beginning to be trained as mountain search and rescue dogs, a role for which they seem eminently suited.

The **Finnish Spitz** is recognized as being the national breed of Finland. There it is a very popular dog, seen everywhere in both town and country. It is one of the

Finnish Spitz

group of Scandinavian spitz breeds which includes the Buhund and the Elkhound. Though an indigenous hunting dog, the Finnish Spitz had almost disappeared from its homeland by the beginning of this century. The purity of the breed was little regarded by anyone until the Finnish Kennel Club realized what was happening and drew up a standard by which the breed should be judged.

Field trials to test the breed's hunting ability are held regularly in Finland. The nickname "Barking Bird Dog" tells us a lot about the Finnish Spitz hunting technique. The dog ranges through the forest ahead of its master, searching chiefly for game birds, in particular various of the grouse family including the capercaillie. Grouse are ground-feeding birds and when the dog scents its prey it flushes them to what appears to be the comparative safety of a tree. Here the bird sits while underneath the dog keeps up a continuous barking, indicating the birds's position to the hunter. Finnish Spitz have very good noses and are occasionally used for tracking other animals, anything from squirrels to moose, but game birds are their real specialty.

Its most remarkable characteristic is the fox-like look given by the bushy, bright red-gold coat. the coat is double for weatherproofing and the woolly undercoat is a lighter shade, giving an almost translucent glow to the reddish brown outer coat. The underparts of the dog shade off into a rich creamy fawn. The eyes are very dark, almond-shaped, and with the lively expression which epitomizes the dog's nature. The bold bearing is typical of the spitz family, as is the bushy tail which curves vigorously forward from its root in an arch held against the thigh. Dogs are about 18in and weigh 36lb.

The **Akita** is one of a number of spitz breeds found in the Far East. The Japanese have at least four such breeds of which the largest, the Akita, is considered the national breed. This is a very imposing and powerful dog with a history of being used to hunt bear, wild boar, sable, and deer. Like many spitz, the Akita is and adaptable animal, being used extensively today for police and army work. Instead of being specialists, the spitz breeds tend to be found in a number of roles and the Akita is no exception. It usually shares the other spitz characteristics of being strong-willed and independently minded. This makes it difficult for the novice owner to handle, especially as the Akita seems rather expressionless compared with many other breeds, and its intentions are therefore less easy to gauge. Akita are dignified dogs whose size commands respect. They make excellent guards.

The breed was unknown outside Japan until servicemen of the American army of occupation saw the dogs and were suitably impressed. Once they reached the show ring in America, efforts were made by breeders to concentrate on rich, clear colors and well-defined markings. Height can be as much as 28in and the body is broad and muscular. The bone should be heavy, with the front leg looking like pillars holding up the wide and deep rib cage. The coat is very dense and double, but the harsh, outer hair is not particularly long, an average of 1½in or so. The breed is aggressive with other dogs.

Akita

The **Chow** is the Chinese version of the spitz type of dog with the short, broad body and the high-set tail carried well over the back that is common to all this group. Early travellers to China mention this dog as used in a variety of ways. The Chow was used for hunting and to haul sleds across muddy land. In many areas it was the general farm dog, killing vermin and guarding property. In some places it was reared and killed for the table. There were superstitions relating to the dog's color and the particular benefits of the flesh of a black or a red dog, and the skins were used for clothing. The first Chows to reach the western world were brought back by the men who sailed to the Dutch East Indies in the 18th century. We know that they were Chows and no ordinary spitz because

Chow

mention was made of the unique feature of the breed – the bluish-black tongue and lining of the mouth. The breed did not, however, become established in the west until early in the century, since when it has become rather more exaggerated in form.

The Chows should have a dignified bearing and a leonine appearance. The ears are small and carried stiffly erect and well forward, a placing that gives the dog a very characteristic scowl. The hind legs are almost straight, which gives the dog a curious gait when viewed from the rear. The minimum height is about 18in. Whole colors alone are accepted, the commonest being red, black, or blue.

Samoyed

The **Samoyed** is one of a number of Spitz breeds found inside the Arctic Circle. These dogs were named after a monadic Samoyed tribe or northwest Siberia who owned them and who regarded them with great esteem, according to the report of 18th–century travellers. The Samoyed dogs herded reindeer, pulled sleds, guarded the tents of their masters, and provided a lot of hair that could be spun and woven into very warm clothing. The dogs had good noses and were able to track straying reindeer and return them to the herd. They also helped to hunt ptarmigan, fox, and sable.

The Samoyed people were well aware of the worth of their dogs, kept them well fed and even allowed them to share their tents during the worst of the winter weather. Fridtjof Nansen, the Norwegian explorer, used Samoyeds on his first polar expedition, and so did Captain Scott on the second attempt to reach the South Pole.

In its native land the Samoyed could be almost any color and the early imports were a variety of shades including black, and black and tan. However, public taste favored the all white specimen and today's standard limits the colors to pure white, white and biscuit, or cream. Dogs should be about 22in in height and should present a strong but graceful appearance. They are active animals, slightly longer in the leg and longer in the back than many spitz. They are an affectionate breed, but very noisy, and they are sometimes aggressive with other dogs. They have a reputation of longevity. There are records of Samoyeds living 20 years or so, an unusual span for any dog.

One of the attractive features of the breed is that the dogs always appear to be smiling. This impression is given by the sparkling brown eye and the fact that the black pigmented lips have an upward curl at the corners, giving the dog a perpetual grin. The Samoyed coat is double with a soft, close, dense undercoat through which the harsh off-standing outer hair grows. To shed snow and ice this outer coat must be stiff and rather coarse. A soft, silky coat is not weatherproof. Properly presented in the show ring the coat almost glistens with a frosty brilliance.

The **Siberian Husky** is another sled dog breed which has come to the fore as a companion animal and show dog since the beginning of the century. Before then they were only owned and bred by the Chukchi peoples who lived a nomadic existence roaming the tundra of northeast Asia. A British naval explorer in the 1850s described the dogs of this tribe as being smaller and wiry, compared with other sled dogs, saying that the sleds they pulled were constructed for speed rather than freight. He described how the dogs' owners could guide them by voice alone.

The gold rush of the Yukon focused a lot of attention on sled dogs. Dog team drivers were proud of their skill, and their rivalry was expressed in racing, the most famous race being the All-Alaska Sweepstake which covered a distance of 408 miles. The fleet dogs of the Chukchi first raced in the Sweep-stake in 1909 under the name Siberian Huskies. Other Alaskan drivers sneered at these lightweight sprinters, but that first team was so impressive that by the next year three teams were entered, coming first, second, and fourth, thus proving conclusively that Siberians not only had speed but stamina as well.

The breed was recognized by the American Kennel Club in 1930 and has since become a very popular dog in America. Not only is it kept as a pet and show dog, but dog-team racing is an even more widespread sport than it used to be. There are a small number of the breed in Britain, where owners are anxious to keep the breed's working ability. The coat of these

Siberian Husky

active dogs is dense and medium in length, often with striking black head markings. Another breed feature are the eyes, which may be brown or a piercing blue, a color appropriate for gazing across icy wastes.

The **Alaskan Malamute** is the heavyweight hauling dog of the north. The Malamute (or Mahlemut) is named after a group of Eskimo people who lived along the shores of the Kotzebue Sound. They were hunters and fishermen who needed hauling dogs strong and powerful enough to tackle the steep and difficult terrain in which they lived. Isolation meant that each Arctic tribe developed its own individual style of sled dog. The same thing occurred with the hunting dogs of Canadian and American Indian tribes. However, once white settlers discovered that the tribal areas were rich enough to be worth invading, these strains of dogs were swamped and lost, as was the culture of their masters. In the case of the Alaskan Malamute the purebred dog barely survived the onslaught of the Yukon gold rush, when hauling dogs became so precious in the north that animals of all types were shipped in. In the resulting cross breeding some indigenous strains of sled dog were permanently lost. Enough typical Malamutes survived, however, to interest exhibitors and breeders, who started showing them at Canadian and American shows in the 1940s.

The mature Malamute can have a height of up to 28in and a weight of 125lb. Such dogs were used as pack dogs during summer hunting trips. They could

Alaskan Malamute

carry up to half their own bodyweight. Single dogs were also used to pull the travois, a simple platform made by lashing a couple of poles together on to which bundles could be tied. As a freight team Malamutes could haul half a ton and keep going day after day in one of the worst climates of the world. Both the men and the dogs who travelled in the Arctic had to be tough, but it should not be forgotten that sled dogs enjoy pulling, and this includes hauling owners along the street, just as much as loads across the snow. They are also dogs who established their position in the team by fighting, so they tend to be aggressive. The usual coloring is various shadings of gray very often with a black cap or mask as a facial marking.

Eskimo Dog

The **Eskimo Dog** is the fourth recognized sled dog breed, though its characteristics are less well defined than the others. Like many true working dogs, as opposed to show dogs, size is very variable, with males being up to 27in in height and 105lb in weight. Color is also variable but the dog has the dignified and independent nature of all the large spitz breeds. They are powerful and liable to be aggressive with other dogs.

The coat is dense, double, and impenetrable to blizzard conditions. Such dogs sleep outside through the worst of Arctic weather. They scrape a small hollow if possible, turn round several times so that their backs are to the wind, and curl up into a ball, letting the snow drift and cover them in an insulating blanket. Sled dogs have fur all over their bodies, including their abdomen and genitals, areas which many other dogs have bare. Once curled up, the only exposed skin, that of the paws and nose, is covered by the plume of the tail and so protected from frostbite.

The **Schipperke** cannot be mistaken for anything but a spitz, despite the absence of a tail. The head, with its erect ears and small, dark eyes, is very fox-like. The name means "little skipper" and the dog acted as a watchdog and rat killer on Belgian canal boats. Its rounded, tailless rump, the thick bushy hair at the back of the thighs, and the longer coat or mane over the shoulders, give it a very distinctive silhouette. The breed is small and compact with a weight of about 15lb, ideal for living in the cramped quarters of a boat. The color is usually black, but can be other whole colors.

Schipperke

Norwegian Buhund

The **Norwegian Behund** was a Jack-of-all-trades on the remoter farms of its homeland: it herded ponies and cattle and acted as a watchdog. Behunds are rather plain, often gray-colored dogs with a homely air. They are about 17¾in in height and often have black on the muzzle and ears, which adds to their look of responsibility. The standard calls for them to be fearless and energetic and, like many spitz, they are also quite vocal. Dogs like these are believed to have sailed with the Vikings, and certainly accompanied the Norwegian settlers who colonized Iceland in 874 A.D.

The **Keeshond** is the Dutch member of the spitz family, one used in the past as a farm guard and as a barge dog on the Dutch waterways. The Keeshond should be a compact and bold dog with brisk, forceful movement. Height is about 18in and the tail should have a double tight curl. The legs are cream in color but the rest of the dog is wolf or ash gray with shading where the lighter undercoat shows through. The coat is somewhat longer than with many spitz but should still be harsh and off-standing. Lighter shading round the dark eyes, the "spectacles," is a unique feature of the breed.

Keeshond

Japanese Spitz

The **Japanese Spitz** is one of a number of small, white, fluffy breeds with little to choose between them except their country of origin. They bear witness to the fact that small, white, long-haired animals have a universal appeal. The Japanese Spitz is some 12in in height and has a long white coat with a profusely plumed tail. It shares the common spitz characteristics of being a very nimble and alert little dog with plenty to say for itself.

A very similar breed is found in Italy where it is known as the **Italian Spitz**. It has always been prevalent in Tuscany, and many Florentine paintings show similar small dogs to have existed there for at least 600 years. If the white coat is of the correct, harsh texture these dogs are easy to keep clean, for dirt should simply brush out.

The **German Spitz** is recognized on the European continent in three sizes, height being the criteria. The *Wolf Spitz* is the largest, with a minimum shoulder height of 18in. As the name indicates the color is wolf gray. The next size down has a minimum height of 16in and the smallest is about 11in. Only whole-colored dogs are accepted: white, black, orange, brown, or gray.

German Spitz

Toy Dogs

The **Pomeranian** is the smallest of the ubiquitous spitz family. Nowadays, this breed is little more than an animated ball of fluff from which a perky little fox face with brilliant dark eyes peers out. Today's dog has been bred for smallness of size and length of coat. The standard advises the weight to be about 4½lb but most show dogs weigh far less. The breed has reached that rather unrealistic position where the bitches shown are often too small to be bred from and the exhibitors keep the larger brood bitches at home, knowing that they are too big to win. Nevertheless most "Poms," even the smallest, are gay and active little dogs, though with a reputation for yapping. Their air of self–importance and the rotundity of their outline given by the wealth of coat constitute a great deal of their charm. The colors are mainly orange and sable. There used to be many others, including black, blue, white, brown, and beaver, allowed to lapse in the constant struggle to get the breed smaller and smaller, and now rarely seen.

Pomeranians are very active little dogs and, being nimble and light on their feet, will take as much exercise as they need, given the freedom of a house and yard. Like all the longer-haired spitz, they need daily grooming with a bristle brush. Start at the head and part the hair so that the coat can be brushed forward from the roots to the tips. Work in strips about an inch wide, repeating the process until the whole of the dog has been covered. With this deep brushing there is little or no need for combing, as mats and tangles do not get a chance to form. Show dogs are trimmed further, the legs and feet in particular being tidied.

The breed takes its name from the area of Germany from which it comes. Paintings by such artists as Gainsborough and Stubbs show admiring owners with white, multi-color and brown spitz weighing about 33lb. A century later Queen Victoria became interested in the breed, making a brown spitz called marco, the gift of the people of Florence, her constant companion. Weighing about 15lb, he would have looked monstrous next to today's tiny dogs.

tots.

Pomeranians

The **Italian Greyhound** is the smallest of the sighthound family, the ideal weight being about 6½lb. It has been said that "the sole difference between Italian Greyhounds and normal 28in exhibition Greyhounds is in the output from their respective interior pituitary glands." Be this as it may, the former does appear as the most delicate miniature of the latter. This dwarfing certainly occurred a very long while ago, since tiny greyhounds were known to the Romans.

A dog whose appearance is so elegant and graceful was bound to attract the attention of those who could afford to keep a dog for pleasure rather than utility. Frederick the Great kept more than 50 of these dainty animals delighting in their company and selecting the people who cared for them with considerable care. Charles I of England, who was known for the love of dogs and censured by the critics for it, knew the Italian Greyhound – his mother, Anne of Denmark, had her portrait painted with five of these little hounds, which look little different from those we see today.

The breed has a very fine coat, thin and glossy like satin. It is therefore a comfort-loving dog, one that would rather be under the blanket than on top. However, it combines this epicureanism with a sporting streak and a turn of speed that leaves no doubt about its place in the greyhound family. Fashion changes as to the most popular color but the only ones barred are dogs with brindle or tan markings. The slenderness and fragility of the dogs'

**Italian
Greyhounds**

appearance suggest a delicate constitution, but this is not the case, though all small dogs are more susceptible to cold and wet than their larger relatives. The final touch of distinction is the Italian Greyhound's high-stepping action.

The main difficulty with Italians is that pencil-slim legs are easily injured, particularly with so active an animal. Litter size is small, as it is with most toy breeds, so these will never be dogs seen on every street corner. One off-putting characteristic is something common to a number of toy dogs, that of shivering under stress. It is always assumed by strangers that the dog is cold, but this is rarely the case. Usually shivering reflects excitement, anticipation, or fear.

73

The **Maltese** appears to be a candy-floss dog sweeping along under a cloud of silky white hair. The action of these small dogs should be sound and free. Size is about 10in high and coat is floor length. Maltese should be sweet tempered, affectionate, and very intelligent as befits a dog whose sole purpose has been as a companion and friend to man since at least 500 B.C. The tail should be carried arched over the back but the plume is so long that it merges into the body hair. The silky straight coat is always white. Since there is no woolly undercoat, as there is in the spitz breeds, and the hair is of such soft texture, the coat hangs straight down, sweeping the ground as the

Maltese

74

dog sails along. The nose is black and so are the eye-rims and lips, making a dramatic contrast to the ice white color. Obviously this mantle of hair requires a lot of care.

Puppies should be accustomed to a daily grooming routine right from the start, even though at a young age they appear to be covered with nothing more than some cotton wool wisps. Teach the puppy to lie on its back first of all, so that you can brush the leg and chest hair softly with a bristle brush. Then stand the dog up and brush in layers, finally using a wide-toothed comb. Accustom your puppy, as soon as the hair is long enough, to having its topknot tied up. Bathing is something that will need to be done frequently. You should remember that all dogs have sensitive skins, sensitive both to over-heated water and harsh washing agents. A shampoo properly formulated for dogs and lukewarm water should be used. Drying must always be thorough, whether you use towels or a hair drier. With so small a dog as the Maltese a human hair dryer is quite adequate, though it is not powerful enough for any of the larger long-coated breeds. All the toy dogs with long hair on their feet need their nails cut, since they will not get enough exercise to wear them down. This is something that should be done often, but only clip the very tip of the nail, since a sensitive nerve runs further down the nail, and cutting into this will be extremely painful for the dog and cause the nail to bleed.

The **Bichon Frise** is a breed which has only recently emerged from obscurity, being recognized by the French Kennel club in the 1930s and the American and British Kennel Clubs in the 1970s. The term "frise" (or curled) refers to the coat, which should have soft corkscrew curls. The texture is fine and silky, and only the feet and muzzle should be slightly trimmed. This is not, in fact, the practice as the Bichon Frise is one of the most sculpted breeds in the show ring. The coat, which is always white, is given a bouffant look by careful scissoring, so that the Bichon resembles a stuffed toy or one of those pajama cases so popular in the 1930s. The minimum length of coat is 2in, and underneath this concealing outline should be a long-necked, deep-chested dog with well-rounded thighs and straight bone.

This should be a happy and lively little dog, enjoying the attention that such a coat needs to keep it in trim. The height should be less than 12in and, sadly for the Bichon, the standard says "smallness being highly desirable." Unfortunately, with dogs, smallness is not always the better, for such animals are often unsound runts with skeletal deformities and reproductive problems. However, perhaps luckily, the Bichon has not had the attention of serious breeders for long enough for its size to have been significantly reduced.

The background to the Bichon's history is a very confusing one. The term Bichon has been used widely to refer to a family of small, long-haired toy dogs who were often white in color and which originated in the

Bichon Frise

Mediterranean basin at least by 500 B.C. This group contains the bichon Maltaise (known in Britain as the Maltese); the Bichon Havanese, which is probably extinct; and the Bichon Teneriffe, which is the old name for the Bichon Frise. As a group, these small white dogs have been extremely popular throughout the ages and, though each breed devotee will claim that it is their particular breed that is being referred to historically, it is not possible to separate the Bichon one from the other with any certainty. This is particularly so when they are dogs that have always lent themselves to exotic and fashionable grooming, a tradition the Bichon Frise obviously upholds.

77

Papillion is the French word for butterfly, a name which epitomizes the lightness and grace of these little dogs, who are members of the European toy spaniel family. More particularly the name is a fanciful reference to the large, heavily fringed, obliquely held ears, which are supposed to resemble the spread wings of a butterfly. For perfection, a narrow white blaze down the head symbolizes the body of the insect. There is also a drop-eared version of this breed, called the **Phalene**, or moth, but this is rarely seen. Papillon have a well documented history from the renaissance onward. Toy dogs were a luxury and status symbol kept by those who had the means. Important people who had their portraits painted dressed themselves in all their finery and included their valued possessions - including their dogs – so in this way we are able to watch the progress of the breed through the centuries. Paul Veronese, the court painters of Louis XIV, and Sir Joshua Reynolds, all included Papillons in the pictures they painted. Today's dog is as graceful, alert, and loving, and as valued by his owners, as those treasured pets of the past.

The breed should not be more than 11in high and should weigh about 6½lb. Papillons are hardy and long-lived and, with proper care, retain their playfulness into old age. They are usually confident and friendly and are easily taught. Quite a number of papillons have taken part in obedience competitions, and they revel in being the center of attention. Quick and light on their feet, they will exercise themselves in a small apartment, yet are active enough to join in country walks.

The Papillon coat is moderately long, fine, and silky. It falls flat on the body but forms a ruff on the chest with the ears, tail, and hind legs being heavily fringed. The tail should be a beautiful plume, carried proudly over the back when the dog trots and streaming out behind, like a banner, when the dog moves at speed. The hair is white with patches that can be any color except pinkish brown.

Papillon

The **Miniature Pinscher** belongs to the Pinscher/
Schnauzer group of breed, all of which evolved in
Germany as closely related types with similar
functions. The Miniature Pinscher is not a modern
breed, for small Pinschers have been known in
Germany since the 16th century. They were probably
not as tiny as today's dogs, whose height should
range between 10 and 12in. However, they were
clean–cut, smooth-haired dogs, full of characteristic
pep and vigor. They were interested in hunting,
chasing, and killing and were kept about the farm and
warehouse in much the way terriers were in England,
to keep down rodents.

Pictures and descriptions dating from the beginning
of the 19th century indicate that the Miniature
Pinscher was already a very smart little dog, it was
suggested by a commentator of that time that both
Italian Greyhounds and the smallest Dachshund had
been judiciously used to reduce size in the Pinscher
and improve quality. From the Dachshund could
have come the clear red coloring, which is much
prized in Germany, and which has led to the breed
being called Reh Pinscher after the roe deer which
abounded in Germany and have the same color.
Black, blue, and chocolate dogs, all with sharply
defined tan markings, are also recognized in the show
ring. From the Italian Greyhound could have come
some of the elegance which distinguishes the
Miniature Pinscher and also the very characteristic
high-stepped gait. Each foot should be lifted high as
if the feet were sprung. This is extremely showy and

Miniature Pinscher

eye-catching but it is also very difficult to breed a sound dog (or horse) with this king of gait.

The breed became established in Britain in the late 1940s. The ears are sometimes cropped to a point. Minature Pinschers have a very high-pitched, screaming bark, which is probably their most unpleasant feature.

81

Affenpinscher

The **Affenpinscher** is the other toy dog among the seven breeds which make up the Pinscher/Schnauzer group. The name means Monkey Terrier, for these dogs have the face and expression of mischievous, little monkey. Their sparkling eyes and prominent chins are framed by a beard, moustache, and topknot of wiry black hair. The coat on the shoulders is slightly longer than that of the rest of the body, where it should be short and rough in texture, needing little care except for brushing. In Germany, where the breed originated, and in America, both ears and tail are cut off but in Britain Affenpinschers are not docked, the natural tail being carried in a curve up over the back. These were once little ratting terriers and are full of curiosity and their own self-importance. In the past they came in a variety of colors but by the 1920s black was considered the only suitable color for the diable comique. As their name implies, they are very playful and active. Being one of the sturdier of the small breeds, up to 11in in height and up to 9lb in weight, the Affenpinscher is large enough to tackle country walks with enthusiasm and yet small enough to be tucked under one arm if needed. They are slow to make friends with strangers and make good watchdogs.

Affenpinscher

The **Australian Silky Terrier** has also been known as the Sydney Silky. Both names tell us of its homeland, where it is a very popular show dog and pet. It made very little impact outside Australia until American personnel, stationed in Australia in the 1940s, saw the breed and took dogs home with them. The American Kennel Club recognized the breed in 1959 with Canada following a few years later. Since then Silkies have become very popular with exhibitors. They reached Britain in the 1970s, and there they are still considered a rare breed. Silkies are one of the four or five breeds created by Australian breeders and are not only the latest in the series, being a mere 80 years or so old, but they are also the only breed created without a utilitarian purpose in mind. They are dogs for the home and the show ring, but have a lot of terrier ancestry behind them which adds a great deal of sparkle and zest to their performance.

Australian Silkies are compact dogs, low set, and of medium length. They should weigh up to 10lb while being only 9in in height but they should have enough substance to suggest that they are capable of killing mice and rats. The keen expression in the small, dark eyes and the strong jaws add to the business-like look. Its coat, however, is the Silky's most distinguishing feature. It should be fine, silky, and with an almost mirror-like gloss. The length is up to 6in and the color in the adult dog should be blue. The shorter hair on the ears, muzzle, and legs is a rich tan.

**Australian
Silky Terrier**

The **Chinese Crested** is one of a very small group of hairless breeds that have always been rare and considered great curiosities. The early history claimed for all these hairless dogs seems to be guesswork, with different authorities mentioning Africa, South America, and the Far East. It is assumed that the hairlessness is some form of incompletely functioning gene, since it seems to be linked with missing molars, but we do not know for certain. Another authority has postulated a blood factor deficiency. What we do know is that the Chinese Crested is the only one of these hairless dogs to have made much impression in the show ring, where it appeals to those who like the esoteric. The skin is soft and smooth to the touch

**Chinese Crested
(Powderpuff)**

**Chinese Crested
(Hairless)**

and can be any color, often delightfully spotted and dappled with bronze, blue, or gray. The color may vary between summer and winter and obviously one has to watch that the dogs do not get chilled or sunburn. The only hair is very fine and silky, a long crest on the top of the skull, feathering on the feet and a plume on the end of the tail. The ears are large and erect and may be fringed with sparse hair.

These are very graceful and affectionate little dogs which weigh about 11lb. Since they lack the insulating properties of a coat they obviously need intelligent care in the respect, but the bonus is that they are odorless and unlikely to leave hairs on the carpet. Many Chinese Crested litters contain coated puppies called Powderpuffs. Their hair is very fine, can be either long or short and has the descriptive title of veil coat. Powderpuffs can be shown and must be used in any Chinese Crested breeding program. Without an infusion of Powderpuff blood the dentition, furnishing, and temperament of the hairless dogs suffer.

The **Chihuahua** is on average the smallest breed of dog in the world, most being between 2 and 4lb in weight. The very tiny ones can weight under 16oz, but this kind of weight is to be avoided: such specimens are often unsound runts with a curious embryonic look that is not typical of the breed as a whole. The smaller the dog the more likely it is to have a molera or fontanelle, where the bones of the skull have not united to form a complete bony casing

Long coat Chihuahua

over the brain. This dangerous condition persists into adulthood in some of the tiny specimens. The more typical dog of average size is usually robust, active, and long-lived. They are little dogs with big personalities: fiery, not to say foolhardy, with other dogs and suprisingly agile. They have the kind of swagger that draws the eye and consequently have been highly successful in the show ring.

The breed was developed in america from small dogs found in Texas, Arizona, and Mexico from 1860 or so onward. The dogs were dubbed Chihuahua after the Mexican state of that name. The type was very varied, and a number of other toy breeds were used to bring size down, add quality, and improve coat. The breed now is divided into smooth coat Chihuahuas and long coat Chihuahuas, these being shown separately but allowed to interbreed, the long coat being recessive to the smooth. The breed should have a well-rounded "apple dome" skull with moderately short nose. The eyes should be full and round, dark in color or with a ruby glow. The ears are large and set on at an angle of 45 which gives added breadth to the skull. The coat can be any color. In smooth coats it is soft and glossy. The long coated dogs have fringed ears, a ruff, feathering in the legs and feet, and a plumed tail. The Chihuahua tail is medium in length but rather flattish and broad in section.

Smooth coat Chihuahua

The **Tibetan Spaniel** is one of two Tibetan breed which are small enough to be considered toy dogs, even though the British Kennel Club does not classify them in that way. Certainly the Tibetan Spaniel is related to the Pekingese, but the exact nature of the relationship is likely to remain a mystery. The Far East has produced a number of snub-nosed small dogs. From pottery, silk paintings, and figurines, we know that such animals were much treasured and also that they have been in existence for well over a thousand years. It was valued as an amusing and cheerful companion and as an alert and vociferous watchdog. There is also the charming story that these spaniels were used to turn the Buddhist prayer wheels, thus ensuring that an endless stream of praise and supplication drifted heavenward.

Type in the Tibetan Spaniel seems to have changed less that it has in some of the other Fare Eastern toy breeds. They are hardy dogs, full of gaiety and animation, but also aloof with strangers as becomes a

Tibetan prayer wheels

Tibetan Spaniels

good watchdog. The head is small in relation to the
body and the muzzle is fairly short and blunt, but not
flattened or wrinkled. The underjaw should be wide
and•prominent and the teeth slightly undershot.
Ideally the drooping ears have long fringes and the
face has a distinctive scowl, caused by the way the
dark eyes are set in the skull. The coat is double but
silky in texture and lies flat on the body. The
Tibetans are reputed to have spun the hair. There
should be a mane or shawl of longer hair over th
shoulders and the richly plumed tail is set high and
carried gaily over the back. The feet are oval and
neat, with feathering between the toes and extending
beyond the nails. All colors are allowable, and the
height is about 10in with quite a wide range of weight
from 9 to 15lb.

91

The **Shih Tzu** is one of at least three breeds with the nickname of "lion dog," and indeed these Chinese words mean lion. The lion plays a very important part in Buddhist mythology, being the animal which is entrusted with the keeping of the jewel of the Law, and was considered the dog of the Buddha himself. The lion was never indigenous to China, so artists using the lion as a symbolic as well as decorative device were able to give free expression to imaginative conceptions of "dog-lions" and "lion-dogs." From the 15th-century onward innumerable versions of the Buddhist lion appeared on Chinese porcelain, wide mouthed, snub-nosed creatures with stylized, wavy flowing hair and a plume of a tail. Both the Tibetans and the Chinese bred small dogs, which by their

Shih Tzus

appearance and lion-hearted temperaments symbolized the lion that was the pet of the Buddha. The Shih Tzu was one such breed, believed to have originated in Tibet and to have reached China in the 16th century, in the time of the Manchu dynasty, when distinguished Chinese officials visiting Lhasa were presented with pairs of these dogs as a mark of honor. A Chinese description of them reads "Lhasa Lion Dog should have lion head, bear torso, camel hoof, feather-duster tail, palm-leaf ears, rice teeth, pearly petal tongue, and movement like a goldfish."

The first three decades of this century saw much confusion among the Tibetan and Chinese breeds. No longer valued in their homelands and not understood anywhere else, the Shih Tzu, the Apso, and sometimes even the Tibetan Terrier were all lumped together under names such as Lhasa Terrier or even Tibetan Poodle. In the 1930s dogs of this type reached Britain, where the shorter-legged, more snub-nosed became known as Shih Tzu. The breed became much more popular in the 1950s and 1960s, both as a pet and as an exhibition animal. They are dogs of amusing and independent character. The beard, whiskers, and the hair growing upward on the nose should give a distinctly chrysanthemum-like effect to the head. The coat can be any color but a white blaze on the forehead is prized. The hair should be long, dense, and straight. Height is about 10in and weight about 16lb.

The **Japanese Chin**, known elsewhere in the world as the Japanese Spaniel, is a demure little dog. It is obviously related to the Pekingese and the other Asian short-faced breeds, but the exact extent of their kinship can only be guessed. The dogs may have been introduced to Japan when monks and teachers brought Zen Buddhism as early as 520 A.D. They became the pets and playthings of the Japanese nobility. Though the Portuguese started trading with Japan in the 16th-century, very few Japanese Chin reached the West. Presumably such treasures were not for sale to Westerners. Commodore Perry, the American naval commander who initiated greater trade between Japan and the West in 1853, actually took Japanese Chin on board for his return voyage. Only two survived, but it was the start of a very brisk export trade. An eye witness account describes Japanese Chin arriving at Australian ports at the beginning of the century, each confined to a handwoven wicker cage as delicately made as the animals themselves.

The breed is still very popular in Japan today. In the West it became fashionable when royalty took an interest in it. Then it was eclipsed by the Pekingese and after two world wars number were low. Since then there has been a resurgence of interest, particularly in the show ring. The Japanese Chin is an essentially stylish dog with a characteristic look of astonishment. It should be dainty, weigh about 7lb and having a profuse coat.

Japanese Chin

The color is predominantly white with either black or red markings.

The **Griffon Bruxellois** is an exception – a toy breed without any aristocratic connections! The breed was developed toward the end of the last century. The little rough-haired terrier types who slept with the horses and killed rats amid the straw of the stables caught the attention of some of the dog fanciers of Belgium. Perhaps it was seeing these little dogs sitting up beside their owners, the cab drivers of Brussels, that sparked off the interest. These Belgian street urchins and the German Affenpinscher (which

95

was then known in a variety of colors) formed the foundation of the breed. A Pug was used to improve the head qualities, giving a more massive skull, shorter nose, and neater ears. The Pug also added to the stockiness of the body, which is such a desirable feature in the Griffon.

Though most puppies were born with rough terrier-like coats, some were now born smooth-coated like their Pug ancestor. These were often looked upon by breeders as being undesirable, until it was realized that these smooth pups had a charm of their own. The smooth variety became known as the **Petit Brabançon**.

In Europe, yet a third variety of Griffon is recognized and all compete separately. In America and Britain, both rough- and smooth-coated dogs compete together in Griffon classes at shows. The

two varieties differ in type and temperament as well as in coat, and the roughs have always been slightly more popular, possibly because the whiskered face has a more devil-may-care expression. Both varieties should look really sturdy, weighing about 11lb.

Most Griffons are red in color with black, and black and tan, making up a substantial minority. The Griffon should still retain its terrier-like disposition and sporting character. It is very four-square in appearance, something that can be emphasized in the roughs by clever trimming. An exhibitor of rough Griffons will be prepared to trim the coat at least twice a year. This involves plucking out the old dead hair with a finger and thumb, and then waiting for the new hair to grow through to the right length before showing the dog again. Thereafter trimming is a continual process until the next bi-annual strip.

Griffon Bruxellois

The **Lowchen** is known in Europe as the Petit Chien Lion, a reference to its traditional styling in the fanciful resemblance of a lion. The breed is unknown in America and was at a very low ebb in Europe until after the Second world War, when interest revived in Germany. In 1971 the first were registered in Britain; numbers have increased quite rapidly since. The Lowchen seems to be related to the small barbers or water spaniels, and to the whole bichon family. It has been in existence for a long time, if one may chart it by following the progress of the traditional clip with the long tufted tail: little lion dogs can be found in most of the great art galleries of Europe in pictures by painters as diverse as Cranach and Goya.

Lowchen in a 15th-century painting

Modern Lowchen

The modern Lowchen is classified as a toy dog but can be up to 13in in height. The dog gives the impression of being strongly built and active with a short, well proportioned body and well muscled hindquarters. The tail should be carried gaily over the back when the dog is on the move. The coat is thick and long, with a fine silky texture. It may be wavy but should not be curly. The hindquarters are clipped out leaving a mane on the forequarters, a tuft on the end of the tail, and bracelets of hair round the wrist and ankle joints. Any color or combination of colors is permissible. The clipped area is often a different shade, forming a tonal contrast to the longer coat,

99

Pug

particularly in brindle or roan and multi-color dogs. These are agreeable little dogs and are easily taught. A number have appeared in the obedience as well as the show ring.

The **Pug** is also considered to be a Chinese breed, but it has been Europeanized for some considerable time. There are accounts and pictures of a smooth-coated stoutly bodied, small dog existing in early China. They are believed to have reached Europe in the trading vessels of the Dutch East India Company in the 16th century. This story is given further substance by the fact that no black Pugs were known until 1880, when Lady Brassey brought several home from a cruise in the Chin areas. The Pug reached

Britain in 1688, when the court of William of Orange came from Holland, accompanied by their fashionable pets. Pugs became 18th–century status symbols. Every lady had to have one. German and French porcelain factories made Pug ornaments which are now valuable collector's items. The pug, even then, kept its tightly curled tail, but its ears were cut off close to its head, for the pain of this was thought to make the wrinkles deeper. At this time all Pugs were apricot or fawn, with a black mask and ears, and often a black trace mark running down the back. The last 100 years has seen black added to the list of colors. The desirable weight is about 18lb. They are a very tolerant and good–natured breed. Their noses are too short for the dog to be able to breathe easily in hot weather.

Pug

The **Pekingese** has become one of the top favorite toy breeds in the West and is yet another breed that is often referred to as a lion dog. This again is because of the Buddhist influence on Chinese culture and the Pekingese, as the name suggests, is a product of the Far East. They were Imperial dogs, bred at the courts of the Chinese Emperors in considerable numbers and always considered too exclusive to be kept anywhere less than the palaces used by the Imperial entourage. The Chinese showed great skill as animal breeders very early on and were particularly interested in the decorative and the grotesque. The small snub-nosed Pekingese with its fanciful resemblance to the Buddhist lion was bred in all sorts of colors which were believed to have symbolic significances. The smaller dogs were of a size that could be carried in the sleeve of Chinese robes and were selected so that their color would complement that of the gown. These exclusive little dogs were not seen, and scarcely heard of, outside Peking until a punitive raid on that capital in 1860 by the British caused the Imperial court to flee. In the hurry and confusion five little dogs were left behind and were sent to England by the officer who found them. One was presented to Queen Victoria, so small that it could sit inside a forage cap. With its scarcity, its royal patronage and its romantic past, the breed was eminently newsworthy. It is, however, the character of the dogs themselves that has kept them so popular.

Pekingese are dogs of unflagging dignity, independent and arrogant, with an enormous self-esteem.

They are adamant in their likes and dislikes, stubborn, yet with the most endearing playfulness for their friends. Any dog so low to the ground with the wealth of coat that a Peke has will need a lot of time spent in daily grooming. The eyes and wrinkled face of all these short-nosed breeds also need daily cleaning to prevent infection.

Pekingese

103

Yorkshire Terrier

Yorkshire Terrier vies with the Chihuahua in having some time individuals, but the majority are a sensible size. The standard allows a weight of up to 7lb, but show dogs are generally about half this. Underneath the very glamorous coat is a compact and strongly made little terrier with plenty of spirit. In pets, the long coat can be trimmed to a manageable length. The coat of an exhibition Yorkshire Terrier is like a glossy silken curtain sweeping the ground. The hair is brushed with the softest of bristle brushes, bathed and oiled so that it does not become brittle and break, and finally is rolled up in protective bundles so that the long strands do not get caught or tangled when the dog is playing or exercising. The yorkie was developed in the north of England in the second half of the 19th century as a ratting dog, possibly by using the now extinct Clydesdale Terrier and the English Toy Terrier. The early dogs were large and coarse by today's standards, but the miners who bred them found a ready sale for the smaller, prettier animals to the manufacturing and mine-owning classes, and size was gradually reduced and quality refined. The coloring of steel blue and rich tan is an important show feature.

The show Yorkie's coat requires grooming and protection.

105

The **Toy Manchester** is the miniature version of the Manchester Terrier. Black and tan has always been favored terrier color and black and tan terriers, with both smooth and rough coats, were well-known among rat catchers and gamekeepers, in the 18th and early 19th century. These dogs varied quite a lot in size, something which still bedevils the show Toy Manchesters today. Dogs as small as 5lb were not uncommon. There is still extant the poster advertising "Tiny, the Wonder, weighing only 5½lbs" whose owner in 1848 bet that his dog could kill 300 rats in less than three hours. Tiny, placed in the rat pit of the Queen's Head Tavern in London, killed this number of rats in just under 55 minutes. The ideal show dog should weigh about 6½lb and be about 12in in height. The breed is smooth, glossy and elegant with an affectionate nature and a natural suspicion of strangers, which makes them good house dogs. The dogs now have an upright ear that should be the shape of a candle flame. They were always cropped in the past and the ban on cropping greatly reduced their numbers, since many of their breeders could not, or would not, adapt to the change in the law. The breed standard calls for the utmost precision in the placings of the rich tan markings on the polished ebony of the coat and this has probably not helped the breed in the show ring.

Toy Manchester. This puppy's folded ears will be erect when it is adult.

The **English Toy Spaniel** is one of two toy spaniel breeds known in Britain. It is a compact little dog with a long silky coat and profuse feathering on legs and tail. This is very often extremely wavy, though this is not considered desirable. The head is massive, with a domed skull and a short nose pushed up at the tip. The most desirable size is about 14lb. Both toy spaniel breeds share the same four color varieties, of which the Blenheim is the most popular, being a pearly white background with chestnut red patches. Particularly important is the white blaze up the forehead, in the center of which should be a small spot of red. It may be a trace of a long forgotten Japanese Chin ancestor, for this mark on the

107

English Toy Spaniel

forehead is greatly esteemed in the breed also, where it is believed to be the thumbmark of Buddha as he blessed the dog. The other colors to be found are tricolor, black and tan, and ruby, which is a whole-colored red.

The **Cavalier King Charles**, one of the most popular of toy breeds in Britain, has yet to make much impact elsewhere. Graceful and active animals who always seem to be pleased with life, their cheerfully waving tails and their affection for the human race have a universal appeal that does much to explain their phenomenal rise in numbers in the last few years.

They have the same four color schemes as the English Toy Spaniel, with whom they share a common ancestry. Cavaliers, however, are more active and sporting in their attitudes toward the world and have a much more typically spaniel head with a tapered, strong muzzle and a flat skull. King Charles I, after whom these toys are named, had small spaniels like today's Cavaliers with long muzzles. These, however, gradually died out as the fashion changed in the 1800s toward a short-faced toy spaniel like today's King Charles. It was left to breeders in the 1920s to recreate the original type and to call them Cavalier King Charles in the memory of their first patron.

Cavalier King Charles Spaniel

Gundogs

English Cocker Spaniels are no longer closely associated with the shooting field but were possibly the earliest spaniel type to be defined and certainly became the most popular. During the 1940s and 1950s Cocker Spaniels were the top dogs in numbers registered in Britain, while at the same period the closely related American Cocker Spaniel was the most popular dog in America. Such success as Companion animals led to a decline in working ability, which was neither wanted nor valued in parent stock. The term

English Cocker Spaniel

American Cocker Spaniel (*see p.112*)

spaniel has been in use since the Middle Ages, but the history of the Cocker Spaniel really starts with the birth of a dog called Obo in 1879. All Cockers can be traced back to him and his influence established the breed, separating it out from the other field spaniels. The commonest theory for the name Cocker is that it arose because these dogs were a suitable size for small game such as woodcock. Cockers have a flat, silky coat with plenty of feathering on legs and ears, and they come in a delightful variety of colors. They are compact little dogs, very strong for their size, which should be about 15in and 31lb. The real appeal of the Cocker lies in its melting expression and the tiny stump of a tail which seems never to stop wagging for an instant.

111

English Springer Spaniel

The **American Cocker Spaniel** is even further from its working past than its English counterpart, starting with exactly the same dog, the Americans developed their own breed and ended up with a gundog. Colors and markings are more important and are very carefully specified in the standard. The head is also very different, the Americans prizing a high domed skull and a short deep muzzle. The coat is of a texture that needs a lot of grooming, if it is not to mat, and a show specimen needs professional clipping to accentuate the dog's neck length and backline and emphasize the generous coat length elsewhere. *Illustrated p.111.*

Some claim the **English Springer Spaniel** to be the oldest of the sporting spaniels. Certainly the name reaches far back into the past, long before the invention of firearms, when spaniels were used to spring or flush game, causing it to leave cover so that the waiting hawks or falcons could stoop at their quarry. Such dogs also sprung birds into nets. Despite the evidence that "springing spaniels" were an early working type, we have no clear idea of what they looked like. By the time shows started in the 19th century, spaniels tended to be separated into land and water spaniels. The former were divided by weight and it is from the heavier classification that the English Springer Spaniel finally emerged. They are still used in the field a great deal, making a very good all-purpose dog for the rough shooting man. For this reason they are not really happy as town dogs, since they are active animals that benefit from a lot of free galloping. The show and working strains in this breed have become very distinct, with the show dog being

Retrieving from water

bigger all round and heavier in bone. The height should be about 20in and the weight some 50lb. Most English Springers are brown and white in color, but black and white and tricolor are equally acceptable. Though still very strong and compact, the English Springer is the highest on the leg and the raciest of all the British land spaniels.

In America the same breed has an altogether different show presentation, illustrating very well how trimming, shaving, and glossing a dog can make it look a quite different animal. The breed is popular in America, but only in the show ring and home. Its niche in the shooting field is occupied by the Brittany Spaniel (p.120), found in large numbers in the United States as a working and field trial dog.

The **Welsh Springer Spaniel** and the Brittany Spaniel share the same ancestry and are possibly of Celtic origin, since these people with their domestic animals settled both areas. The earliest records of the Laws of Wales are believed by breed devotees to refer to the Welsh Springer when they state that a spaniel was of equal value to the King's buckhound. They have always been highly regarded in Wales as working dogs, being expected to help about the farm as well as hunt the hedgerows for the guns. There are still a number of unregistered strains of undoubted antiquity in the smaller, less frequented Welsh villages. The Welsh is a very distinctive spaniel and this particular type can be picked out with some certainty in the sporting prints of the 18th century and some of the family portraits painted by such artists as John Copley and Joseph Wright. The coat is flat and silky, less profuse on the ears and legs than some other spaniels, and always pearly white with rich red patches. The coat stays naturally fairly clean, which may be due to its oiliness, for this dog is also a very keen retriever from water, where an oily coat helps to keep a dog dry. The ears are an unusual shape, something like a vine leaf, and covered with short feathering. Welsh Springers make excellent workers, but their good noses may lead them into trouble when hunting unless they are taught obedience at an early age.

Welsh Springer Spaniel

The **Clumber Spaniels** are the heavyweights of the spaniel world, massive, benign, and deceptively slow-moving until you want to catch up with them. Basically all spaniel work is the same. The dogs are bred to search for either furred or feathered game, and for this they need very good noses. They have to flush the animals they locate out into the open for the guns to shoot. This means that they have to be dogs that will face thickets and thorns, bramble patches, and gorse, with enthusiasm, their delight in searching making them indifferent to scratches and cuts. Once the animal or bird has been shot the spaniel has to

Clumber Spaniels

find where the body has fallen and bring it back to its master. This means that they have to be biddable, easily taught, so that they are controllable in the field. They must not chase whatever it is they have so painstakingly found. They must sit instantly at the sound of a shot and wait until ordered to find and retrieve.

Different spaniel breeds have been developed for different terrain and to suit individual owners' requirements. The Clumber Spaniel is a case in point. It is a very heavy dog with a large, square head for pushing through heavy undergrowth, such as thickets of rhododendrons. It has a large, square, pink nose and bushy brows which help to protect its eyes when it is working with its head down. The long, heavy, and powerful body is like a battering ram. The dog is not built for speed, nor were the sportsmen who used the Clumber in its heyday as a working dog. These were often Edwardian gentlemen, mature in years and slowed down from their boyish enthusiasm by many years of good living. They could afford to take their time and enjoy the patience and persistence shown by Clumbers when working. Today the fashion is for faster working spaniels who can cover more open ground at a quicker pace. The Clumber is now seen only at shows, where a small band of faithful enthusiasts keep it going. The dog weighs about 70lb. The coat is close and silky, always white but with yellow markings and freckles on the muzzle.

The **Sussex Spaniel** is another rairity. As the name indicates it was a dog bred and used locally in the English county of Sussex. The breed was the creation of one man, Mr. Fuller of Rosehill Park, and he wanted a dog that would hunt slowly through thick gorse and bramble. The Sussex is also a beetle-browed dog, strongly built but not so massive as the Clumber. The weight should be about 45lb and the height 16in. It is believed that the Sussex today is a smaller dog than a century ago and this may be due to the in-breeding necessitated by the breed's low numbers. The Sussex's method of working is unusual. Where other spaniels are silent, the Sussex was expected to make noise or bark when on the scent. Experienced owners could tell whether the dog was after fur or feather by the dog's tone. Sussex are always a splendid rich golden brown in color, with each hair shading in gold at the tip.

Sussex Spaniel

Field Spaniel

The **Field Spaniel** is one of the rarest and the plainest of spaniel breeds. It is probably in better shape now than it has been for 50 years, but its position is still fairly precarious. The breed has an ancestry similar to that of the Cocker, and early spaniel classes were simply for "Field Spaniels Over 25lb" and "Field Spaniels Under 25lb." By 1892 the two breeds separated and Field Spaniel breeders proceeded to make it a very exaggerated dog in length. By the time that this had been corrected the Cocker had stolen the limelight and the Field has never really come out of the shadows. It is a working dog of unusual docility. Strongly built, it should weigh about 50lb and stand about 18in at the shoulder. The Field Spaniel should be a whole-colored dog and is usually black or brown.

119

The **Brittany Spaniel** is the bridge between the spaniel and the setter groups. Spaniels work within range of the gun and flush birds within that range. This works well where density of cover can hide a lot of game. Where the ground is more open, in moorland conditions for example, a faster, lighter dog is required that has a much bigger range. Such animals are the pointers and setters which, traveling fast, quarter the ground in front of the guns, sniffing for the scent of hidden birds. Obviously, such dogs will often find sitting birds when they are some distance from the guns. When they do, they "point" or "set" the birds, freezing into a rigid posture that not only indicates the bird's position but also endeavors to pin birds down until the guns can come within range. The Brittany Spaniel is the only spaniel breed that points, and one can see immediately that it is faster than the other spaniel breeds.

The Brittany Spaniel developed in the area whose name it bears. The sporting French created a large number of hunting breeds, each confined to only a small locality. In the 19th century British sportsmen crossed to Brittany to shoot woodcock, taking their own sporting dogs with them, particularly setters. It is from a mixture of this blood and the local Breton spaniel type that the Brittany Spaniel finally emerged. Today's dog works equally well in woodland and water, and ranges far and fast enough to locate upland birds such as quail. It is possible the latter ability that has made them into an extremely popular gundog in America, where they are even more widely kept than in France.

Brittany Spaniel

The Brittany is rarer a square dog with the height at the withers – about 20in – being equal to the length from the withers to the root of the tail. The latter may be missing altogether, naturally short or artificially docked. The original coat color was orange or red on a white base, although black and white is also allowable. Weight is about 45lb. The eyes are amber with a pinky-beige nose and eye rims, which gives the dot a rather hard, staring expression.

German Shorthaired Pointer

The **German Shorthaired Pointer** is a dual purpose gundog, expected to point and retrieve, and is one of a number of such breeds developed in Europe and subsequently exported. It should not be forgotten that these are still working dogs first and foremost, and this does much to account for their great success in America, where hunting and field trialling play a large part in sportsmen's lives. The breed was developed from the German Pointer, a calm, slow-working dog with an excellent nose. Speed, style, and enthusiasm were added to this base by using English Pointers and possibly the Bleu de Gascogne. The German Shorthaired Pointer will range the quarter at speed, follow a trail with persistence, and retrieve under the most difficult conditions. Dogs are about 70lb and 25in. The coat is short, flat, and course. The color is either solid brown, brown and white ticked or flecked, or the same type of patterning in black and white.

The **German Wirehaired Pointer** was also deliberately created at the beginning of this century by German sportsmen. The rough coat of the dog, together with its love of water and its tolerance of icy conditions, probably come from the Pudel Pointer in its ancestry. The guarding instinct, the suspicion of strangers, and the courage in tackling large and dangerous quarry may perhaps be attributed to the Airedale Terrier, which was also used at the beginning. It is not common outside its homeland where it is often used as a gamekeeper's dog, hunting wild cats and foxes.

**German
Wirehaired
Pointer**

The **Vizsla** is one of a number of very distinctive
breeds originating in Hungary. This, too, is expected,
to be an all-purpose gundog, one capable of finding
the game, indicating where it is, and bringing it back
when it is shot. It is an active and intelligent dog,
affectionate, sensitive, and therefore anxious to please
and easy to train. It is a robust dog with a weight of
66lb and a height of 25in. The head is described as
being gaunt and noble with well-developed nostrils
and strong and powerful jaws. The eye should be a
shade darker than the coat color and the ears are long,
thin, and pendulous, a common feature in most
breeds with excellent noses for tacking. The body is
muscular and the dog has rather a racy appearance,
partly due to the prominent breastbone and partly to
the proportions of leg length to body length. The tail
is rather low set and only two thirds are left on. The
coat is short, dense, and coarse, and should feel oily
to the touch, as befits a dog who should work in
swamp and marsh and enthusiasm. One of the most
attractive features of the Vizsla is its color. It is always
russet gold, a shade which glows in sunlight. It is a
very popular dog in Hungary and reasonably well
established in America and Britain. However, its close
working style does not suit the American sportsmen as
well as some of the more far-ranging of the European
gundogs, and it has not achieved the popularity here
that might have been expected.

A Vizsla type of dog appears to have existed from
the 18th century onward and it is suggested that it
shows the influence of a cross with one of the Central

Vizsla

European whole-colored hounds and one of the Balkan pointers. The Vizsla was bred to hunt the great plains of Hungary which teemed with game: deer, hare, duck, geese, and upland game birds such as partridge and quail. The dog therefore is not a specialist hunter but needed to be much more versatile. It is trained to search thoroughly within gunshot rather than to quarter widely, will also track over long distances, and is an accomplished and enthusiastic retriever both from water and land.

The **Weimaraner** is one of a handful of "once seen, never forgotten" breeds for it is a very distinctive silver gray dog. The coat should almost have a metallic sheen and this, together with the breed's yellow or blue-gray eyes, have given them the nickname of "ghost dogs." The color is unique among dogs and gives no clue to the dog's ancestry. A gray dog of similar type appears in a Van Eyck portrait. Two centuries later the Grand Duke of Weimar was developing the gray hunting dog which now bears his name. This was a very exclusive dog kept only by the Duke and given to such of his court as were prepared to follow his breeding policy. After another 80 years, the Weimaraner Club of Germany was founded, with the same exclusive policies designed to protect the breed. Forty more years were to pass before the first Weimaraner left Germany for America, where attempts were made during the 1930s and 1940s to keep the breed equally exclusive. The breed reached Britain in the 1950s, just when numbers were really taking off in America, where they became very popular.

The Weimarener standard states that the dog's hunting ability is the paramount concern, and as a gundog and worker the breed is much used in the United States. However the Weimaraner is a dog with other talents. The temperament should be fearless friendly, protective and obedient, and this does much to explain why the dog also excels at obedience work, working trials, and has made its debut as a police dog.

Weimaraner

The **Pointer**, that most elegant of specialist gundogs, is the product of the skill of British sportsmen in breeding a dog of style and symmetry. There are many kinds of pointers across Europe (France has at least five) but the Pointer is always the British dog, the only one so well known that it needs no further descriptive title. It was a dog whose skill was so preeminent in its field that it was used to improve many other breeds of gundog or to form the basis for new breeds. We know that the Spanish Pointer reached England at the beginning of the 18th century. This was a slow, ponderous dog with and excellent nose. Its pace suited those still coping with muzzle loading guns. As sporting guns improved and people were able to shoot flying birds with some degree of success, instead of having to shoot them while they

Pointers

roosted, faster and more talented gundogs were needed.

Opinions differ as to what was grafted on the old Spanish stock but, by the time dog shows started in 1859, the Pointer was already a classic of a dog. The head and skull are one of the hallmarks of the breed, for the muzzle should be slightly concave. The dog is built on galloping lines and is seen at its best in the open country it needs to work. The short, hard coat is usually white with orange, yellow, brown or black markings and the height is about 27in. With the break up of big sporting estates fewer Pointers are worked in Britain than ever before, but the converse is true in America, where they are a popular hunting dog and run in many field trials.

The **Irish Setter** is one of the breeds so well known and liked that it has acquired a nickname by which it is better known than the original – that of Red Setter. It is an immensely popular dog on both sides of the Atlantic. Films and books based on the Red Setter have given the breed a further boost, and numerically it has far outstripped the other two setter breeds. As with most of the Irish breeds, little is known about the Setter's origins. We know it existed in the 18th century, used by the Irish gentry to find the game on their big estate. Irish Setters are obviously dogs built to gallop all day but they have always had the reputation for being rather headstrong and scatter-brained. Certainly very few are used for work of any description today. They are kept instead for their glamorous looks and their affectionate nature.

The standard description says the Irish Setter should be racy, full of quality, and kindly in expression. It is the melting expression of the eyes that is one of the breed's charms. The eye-catching color, from which the nickname comes, is a rich glowing chestnut red. The coat is silky, flat to the body, and very glossy, with abundant feathering on the tops of the ears, the legs, and the tail. A century ago the Irish was not always a red dog, and in Dublin before 1877, Irish Setter classes were divided by color with White and Red Setters being in the majority. Today the Red and Whites are being revived as a separate breed, a more workmanlike and less glamorous dog.

Irish Setter

Irish Red and White Setter

131

Gordon Setter

The **Gordon Setter** is the only native Scottish gundog and takes the name from the Dukes of Gordon, who developed the breed. It has never been a very popular breed as a show dog or a pet but has a respectable record as a working gundog. In particular the Gordon Setter Club of America has taken great pains to foster the working image. Gordon Setters are at their best when doing the job for which they were bred, finding game birds, particularly grouse, on the moors. Out of this environment they are less ebullient than the other setter breeds, taking little interest in the show ring unless patiently coached by their owners.

They are dignified dogs, very anxious to please the one person to whom they are deeply attached. They greet their friends gravely and are reserved with strangers. From the exhibitor's point of view they also suffer from being a slow breed to mature. All the slow-maturing breeds need care in rearing since the temptation is always to push them on too fast. While the young dog is still at that uncoordinated gangling stage it still needs plenty of good food and a controlled amount of exercise.

The Gordon, when mature, is a very strong dog of exceptional stamina. They are about 26in in height and should weigh 65lb. The breed is required to have style and is compared to a weight-carrying hunter rather than a racehorse. The head is deep rather than broad, with lean cheeks and a fairly long muzzle whose depth is accentuated by the upper lip hanging loosely over the lower. The eyes should be dark brown and bright. The ears are set low on the head, are of medium size, and thin in texture. The tail should be carried horizontally and is on the short side, not reaching below the hock. The coat should lie flat against the body, by moderately long, silky in texture, and a deep, shining coal back. The tan markings should be a lustrous, ripe horse-chestnut color. When a mature dog is presented to perfection this coloring can be very striking. The old name for the Gordon Setter was the Black and Tan Setter. There is a reference to these in Scotland as far back as 1726, but their history is a breed really starts with the Duke of Gordon's strain some 30 years later.

The **English Setter** should be a very friendly and quiet natured dog. All the setters are expected to do the same kind of work in the shooting field and all are believed to have descended from the setting spaniels known and described in the Middle Ages. These dogs searched for game and either crouched or sat when the scent told them they were near birds. Such setting spaniels were longer in the leg than today's spaniel breed and worked with the same lashing tail as the setters do when quartering the ground. Setting dogs in England have an unbroken history back to the 13th century. The original long-legged spaniel was probably crossed with a pointer at some later stage, and in the 19th century the English Setter was improved tremendously, both in looks and performance, by two men who devoted a great deal of time and skill to the breed. So distinctive were the strains they bred that they became known briefly as Laverack Setters and Llewellyns.

Today's English Setter is no longer used as a gundog in Britain. In the United States, the breed has split into the working type and the show type. The former are small, lightweight, plain dogs with enthusiasm for their work. Beside them the show English Setter is statuesque, relaxed, and well-mannered. It is also larger, heavier, and carries more coat. As it has always attracted plenty of admirers, the loss of the breed as a working dog in Britain need not be too serious. Height can be 27in and weight 66lb. The English Setter tends to be slightly shorter on the leg than either of the other two setter breeds; this is

English Setter

because it was worked mainly on grassland and
stubble, rather than moorland or bog. The coat is flat
and silky, with well feathered legs, lower chest and
tail. The color is mainly white with flecks and freckles
of blue, or orange, or brown or black. The delicate
dappling and the shading of these colors are one of
the English Setter's chief attractions. Solid, heavy
patches of color are not considered desirable. The
eyes should be bright, mild, and intelligent, giving the
dog a benevolent look.

The **Large Munsterlander** is an all-purpose gundog developed in Germany at the beginning of this century. This is a breed that is both worked and shown by enthusiasts in France and Germany, and one that is just gaining a foothold in Britain, although it is still relatively unknown in the United States. British owners are equally keen to keep the breed's working qualities. It is supposed to be ideal for the rough shooting man and is very enthusiastic, not to say impetuous in the field. In Germany the quarry includes fox, hare, and roe deer, the dog works equally well retrieving from water as from land. The breed is always black and white and resembles a lightweight setter. Dogs should be about 25½in high. The drive and energy of the breed makes them unsuited to urban life.

Large Munsterlander

Italian Spinone

The **Italian Spinone** acts as a pointer in its native land, searching out and indicating the presence of game by that sudden freezing of movement that makes the dog look as though it has been transfixed. The breed, or local varieties of it, seems to have existed in the north of Italy for some centuries. The Spinone is a solid, vigorous-looking dog, strongly boned and muscled. It is a big dog, 27in in height and about 82lb in weight and, by its build, obviously not designed to be particularly speedy. However, the Spinone has tremendous endurance and is a good tracking dog. The coat is course and wiry, usually white with lemon or brown patches or flecks.

137

The **Flat-coated Retriever** is enjoying a modest and well deserved revival in Britain due to the publicity gained when one of this breed went Best in Show at Crufts Show in 1980, it is now also gaining in popularity in the United States. The Flat Coat, and indeed all retrievers, were created in the 19th century in response to the changes in the shooting field. Up to that time, pointers and setters had found birds and, after they were flushed and shot, were often expected to retrieve them as well, which they did in a rather unenthusiastic and haphazard manner. A number of factors emphasized the need for specialist retrieving dogs. The management of estates improved and so

Flat-coated Retriever

did the accuracy of guns, so that the number of birds killed and wounded during a day's shooting became larger. It became essential to have dogs that would track wounded game and find and collect the dead from all sorts of undergrowth and cover.

Victorian sportsmen were great experimenters, trying all sorts of crosses between breeds, some of them successful and some not. The Flat-coated Retriever is believed to have come from some Setter/Labrador combination. It was originally called the Wavy-coated Retriever, which supports this hypothesis. It became the most popular of the retrievers by the end of the century but by the 1920s had been totally eclipsed by the Labrador and Golden. The Flat Coat is a very hardy, robust and trouble-free animal, kindly in disposition and easily taught. The weight is about 70lb and the color of the dense coat is black or brown.

The **Curly-coated Retriever** is the largest of the retriever group and certainly one of the earliest to be developed. The dog's most distinctive feature is its coat, which should be one mass of crisp, small curls all over, except for the muzzle and skull which are smooth. This coat is thick, traps air as an insulating layer when the dog is in the water, and is a good protection against thorny undergrowth. The fur is slightly oily and the wetter the coat, the tighter the curl - which is why exhibitors can be seen watering their Curlies before they take them into the show ring. The desirable height at the withers is 27in, and

139

Curly-coated Retriever

this is a strong, smart, upstanding dog with plenty of stamina. The color is either black or brown and the dog has a nice dark eye to match the coat. This is another slow-maturing breed, with youngsters remaining gawky for quite a long period.

The Curly Coat has a number of sides to its character and is rather more of a guard dog than the other retriever breeds. It has also been trained successfully as a guide dog for the blind. Despite its charm, the Curly Coat has never been a popular dog in the 20th century, though it was well thought of at the end of the 19th. The Curly Coat is obviously related to the water spaniel and poodle groups, and shares their enthusiasm for swimming.

The **Chesapeake Bay Retriever** is the American retrieving breed, little known elsewhere in the world. It is supreme at its job, which is retrieving duck from the icy waters of Chesapeake Bay. It is a hard-headed, aggressive, really tough dog, with the courage and stamina to face freezing water again and again and again during a long day's waterfowling. The coat is decidedly oily and therefore very pungent when wet. The hair is short, thick, tough, and slightly wavy. The color is very distinctive, being described as "deadgrass." In practice this means shades of faded tan through to a dull tobacco brown. Dogs can be up to 26in in height and 75lb in weight.

Chesapeake Bay Retriever

The **Labrador Retriever** can in some ways be considered a British breed, since the dogs, now spread worldwide, all stem from British stock. However, as the name suggests, the breed originated on the wild and rocky coasts of Labrador and Newfoundland. There, where fishermen sailed out of tiny, inaccessible harbors to catch cod off the Newfoundland Banks, working dogs were part of the everyday scene. They were in and out of the sea the whole time, helping haul ashore the heavy nets, the dripping tow line, the drifting oar, and the fish that had slid over the gunwhales.

Writers mentioning these dogs in the 1840s called them St. John's Dogs, after the capital of Newfoundland, and to distinguish them from the Newfoundland dog proper. However, a letter to the magazine *The Field* in 1869 says "Around St. John's are great numbers of smooth-haired black dogs from 18in to 24in high called Labradors" and from then on the name stuck. The dogs arrived in Britain on the fishing boats that were their homes. Each boat might carry a couple of dogs, curled up out of the way among the ropes and gear, ready to fetch anything that might be lost overboard. The dog's usefulness was noticed by the people buying the fish cargo when the boat reached the southern British ports such as Poole, and the dogs were sold as well as the cod. Sportsmen, too, began to appreciate that such a dog would be invaluable from wild-fowling and, by the end of the 1800s, the Labrador retriever was established as a working gundog in Britain at a time

Labrador Retriever

when it had virtually disappeared in its homeland owing to a punitive dog tax.

The Labrador is one of the most popular of breeds, not only as a gundog but also as a guide dog for the blind and as a family pet. The thick, short, dense coat is generally either black or yellow, though other whole colors such as chocolate sometimes appear. Up to 22½in in height, the breed is sturdy, active, and strong. A sensible, well behaved Labrador is a joy, but they do need training to prevent them from becoming too boisterous and nuisance to others. If you are thinking of buying a Labrador, remember that they are dogs bred to work in water and that they like being wet and muddy.

The **Golden Retriever** should be an active and sound dog. The skull should be broad with a wide and powerful muzzle, as becomes all the retrieving breeds. To find, pick up, and carry over obstacles and through brush such animals as hares, ducks and geese, a dog not only needs to be strong but also needs jaws that are big enough to hold its burden. The dog is also required to be soft-mouthed, so that it retrieves without marking its bird. The feathers should be barely ruffled and certainly nothing like a tooth mark should pierce the skin. So deeply is the desire to use their mouths bred into retrievers that many have the delightful habit of bringing their owners a "present" as a greeting, rushing off to find a shoe or a toy and bringing it back with obvious pride and satisfaction. Both the Golden Retriever and the Springer Spaniel are prone to greeting their owners in this way.

The Golden is a dog with a particularly kindly expression, a gentle and biddable dog, with a great family loyalty, especially with children. The coat should be dense and water resisting, either flat to the body or slightly wavy. There should be plenty of feathering on the back of the legs and fringing the tail. The color should be any shade of gold or cream Goldens do seem to have got very much lighter over the years and it looks as though the name may end up a misnomer. In America, where the breed is quite popular, cream is not an allowable color in the show ring. The Golden Retriever is not an aggressive dog under any circumstances, and its equable temperament has made it invaluable for the Guide Dogs for the Blind Association which trains a large number of Golden Retrievers. The breed also figures heavily in the Association's breeding program.

The breed as we know it today was developed in the kennels of Lord Tweedmouth during the 1860s. As he kept very accurate kennel records, we know that his foundation stock was a yellow retriever dog and two Tweed water spaniel bitches. The latter breed is now extinct, so we know little of its appearance. Goldens were first registered as a color variation of the Flat Coat but achieved separate breed status in 1913.

Golden Retriever

The **Irish Water Spaniel** is one of a group of water dogs that share a common ancestry. However, details seem to be almost totally lacking of the precise relationship between these breeds. All we know is that water dogs and water spaniels are frequently mentioned by all sorts of writers from Tudor times onward. This type of animal was very useful and very widespread, but few references contain any description or illustration until we come to Thomas Bewick's *Quadrupeds* in 1790. His water dog has a long shaggy coat, like the French Barbet, and his water spaniel has "its hair beautiful curled or crisped." This feature is the first thing one notices about the Irish Water Spaniel, a hard working, powerful dog for finding and retrieving game in marsh and bog.

This is a spaniel for the wildfowler, an enthusiastic dog where water is concerned and an animal with an

Irish Water Spaniel

American Water Spaniel

excellent nose. The coat is dense, pungent – smelling, and covered all over with crisp curls, except for the face and three-quarters of the tail, which are covered with short smooth hair. The curly hair grows into a peak on the top of the skull, an interesting pattern which is found only in one or two of the other water spaniels and the Curly-coated Retriever. The Irish Water has an extravagant topknot of longish curls, and the coat is always a dark brown with almost a purplish look. Height is about 23in and weight is not given.

The **American Water Spaniel** is still very much of a working dog, shown very little and unknown outside the United States. It is a smaller dog than the Irish Water – height 18in, weight 40lb – but has the same pattern of hair growth on the head. The closely curled

147

coat is either brown or dark chocolate, and the American Water's larger ear and smaller size suggest that something like the Cocker Spaniel is an ancestor.

The **Portuguese Water Dog** is another with a coat of short, dense curls – or at least one type is, for this is a breed with two coat types. The other version has a long, wavy coat. The Portuguese Water Dog is a fisherman's dog from the Algarve. It was possibly never very numerous, and modern fishing methods have led to a further decline. However, it is a breed that has always had rather a romantic image and, being a working dog that has been known for some centuries, a handful of enthusiasts are endeavoring to keep it in being. America, in particular, has a club looking after the breed's interests.

Basically, this is a retrieving dog, one that was expected the fetch anything that fell overboard, from oars to ropes or slippery fish. They were also used as couriers from ship to ship, or ship to shore. They were expected to guard their master's boats and gear but, unfortunately, are also rather quarrelsome with other dogs. The height is about 22in and the weight 55lb. The color can be black, or brown, or white, or a mixture of any two of these three. The breed, when shown, has the hindquarters clipped out and a plume left on the end of the tail in a style similar to the Lowchen. It presents a very elegant silhouette when trimmed and groomed in this way, and apparently was often trimmed like this for work, as were other breeds of dog used for retrieving from water. There

Portuguese Water Dog

does not seem to have been a logical explanation for the Portuguese trim, and it is possibly nothing more than a local fashion.

The **Poodle** was originally another retrieving breed, a sporting dog with a fondness for water. The poodle trim, with a bouffant mane left on the front end of the dog whilst most of the hair is cut from the hindquarters, may be a relic from the time when the dog spent a lot of time in the water. Some people suggest that the air trapped in the dog's mane kept it buoyant; others that clipping the hindquarters prevented the dog being dragged down by a mass of wet coat. Since these theories contradict each other, a logical reason for the tim has yet to be found. The

149

Poodle has long left its sporting past behind and is today one of the most popular, vivacious, and fun-loving of companion animals. There are three Poodle breeds, divided only by size, the requirements being slightly different in different parts of the world.

The oldest and the largest Poodle breed is the **Standard Poodle**, often over 22in in height. These extrovert dogs in the full show clip make a magnificent

**Standard Poodle
(lion clip)**

Toy and Miniature Poodles

spectacle. However, their size, and the amount of grooming involved, limits their appeal. The next size down, the **Miniature Poodle**, under 15in, was developed early in this century and became immensely popular until overtaken by the youngest of the three breeds, the **Toy Poodle**, under 11in, in the 1950s. The poodle coat is very profuse and should be harsh. Grooming and trimming must take up a lot of their owner's time if the dog is to remain clean and comfortable. All sorts of clips have been evolved for the pet dog but the lion clip is traditional for the show ring. Poodles are whole-colored dogs, coming in a wide range of pastel shades as well as black, white, and brown.

151

The **Dalmation** is a strong, active, and muscular dog whose symmetry of outline suggest a fair turn of speed. They are dogs of athletic and unexaggerated build that the capable of great endurance. They are not a dog for owners faint-hearted about exercise. The dog's coat makes it an instantly recognizable breed. The ground color is always pure white and the dog is spotted all over with round, well defined, evenly spaced spots. These are usually black, in which case the dog will have a black nose and a dark, sparkling eye. It is equally correct for the dog to have brown spots, in which case it will have a brown nose and amber eyes. The placing of the spots is considered very important. They should not run

Dalmatian

together in blotches and should be smaller on the extremities than on the dog's body. Curiously, the puppies are born white and the sports begin to appear as shadowy patches on the coat when the litter is about two weeks old. The coat itself is short, hard, and dense and should present a sleek and glossy appearance which only needs the minimum of daily grooming. The height can be as much as 24in and the weight about 55lb.

The Dalmatian's origins are not known but there is plenty of evidence from the 17th century onward that it was widely known and kept in Europe. Spots have always been an attractive feature to animal breeders. Even the ancient Egyptians established a spotted breed of dog. There are romantic stories that the breed is a gypsies' dog and comes from Bengal, or that it evolved in the area of the Adriatic from which it takes its name. Whatever the truth, but the 1600s the Dalmatian was appearing as a gundog in hunting pictures, and as a household companion in Dutch genre paintings. A century later the Dalmatian was known as a coaching dog, kept in the stables and exercised with the horses. The dog ran under the axle of the carriage, or sometimes preceded the horses, and was considered and elegant attendant to a fashionable equippage. There are accounts of them covering 16 miles in an hour. The dogs were very often cropped and wore the wide brass collars then in vogue. In America the breed became associated with horse-drawn fire engines and is still known as the "fire house" dog.

Giant Breeds

The **Newfoundland** is another water dog but of a very much larger size and different type from the retrievers and spaniels. The Newfoundland should impress the eye with size and strength and massive bone. It should not, however, appear inactive, but should more freely, giving the impression of being light on its feet. The average height is about 28in and dogs can weigh as much as 150lb. As with many large breeds, Newfoundlands are dignified type, not too keen on being hurried or pushed around. Though gentle and docile, they are also determined and have minds of their own. They are exceptional swimmers, faster than one would expect, and very powerful. They have and impressive record of saving people in difficulties in the water and each year water trials are

Landseer Newfoundland

Newfoundland

held for the breed to ensure that the aptitude is not lost. The coat is flat, coarse, and dense and has an oily nature. The usual color is black, but brown

Newfoundlands are acceptable. The black and white variety is called a Landseer and is regarded as a separate breed in Europe. This is a white dog with black patches, striking to look at but difficult to breed with symmetrical markings.

Newfoundlands come from the island of that name, where they were used for haulage as well as water work. They pulled loads of firewood from the interior, dragged loads of fish to the drying racks, and hauled dripping nets from the sea. Like the Labrador, they lived as much in the sea as out.

The **Great Pyrenées Dog** is one of a number of giant breeds developed as guard dogs in Europe. All of these call for responsible ownership, since their large size and strong territorial sense can be a liability, unless it is firmly under control. Both temperamentally and physically all the giant breeds mature rather late, certainly past the age of two. With dogs of this size, who so rapidly become too big to be manhandled easily, simple obedience training has to be started very early and the rudiments taught before the dog reaches six months of age.

The Great Pyrenées should possess size and substance and has a certain air of majesty. The minimum height is 28in and minimum weight is 110lb but most individuals are much larger than this. The head should be carried high and should give an impression of elegance and strength without coarseness. The eyes are almond-shaped and dark amber brown. The roof of the mouth, the nose, the eye rims, and the lips should all be black. The tail is thick and long, heavily plumed, and has a slight curl at the tip. The coat is double with a woolly undercoat and a coarse, thick, straightish outer jacket. The color is either white or mainly white with patches of gray, yellow, or black and white on the head and at the root of the tail. The Great Pyrenées is one of those breeds where all-white breeding is believed to lead to a certain degeneracy with lack of correct pigmentation and smaller size creeping in, unless dogs with patches of color are used at intervals. The Great Pyrenées carries the coat it does because it was a dog whose

**Great Pyrenées Dog
wearing a protective collar**

function was to guard the mountain flocks of sheep. Such dogs never went under a roof and needed the same protection from the weather as the sheep get from their fleece. The dogs ran in pairs, prepared to attack wolves or thieves, both more common on the Pyrenées then than now, and wore iron spiked collars to protect their throats. By the 18th century Great Pyrenées had become better known and were being used to guard chateaux and country estates. Double dewclaws on the hind legs are a special feature of this breed.

157

The **St. Bernard**, like a number of the giant breeds, is very popular in America, where more people have the space to cater for very large dogs. Size and substance are very important, with a minimum height of 28in. Many are much bigger than this, up to 34in and weights have been recorded of more than 220lb. These should be dogs of kindly benevolence and immense dignity, but some tend to be rather ponderous, as if their weight had outgrown their strength. There are two coats in the breed, the rough, which is popular in Britain, and the smooth, which is popular in the United States. The color is either orange

Smooth St. Bernard

Rough St. Bernard

or red-brindle or mahogany-brindle, all with white. The face and ears very often have black shading.

From about 1670 the dogs were used by the monks of the Hospice of St. Bernard in the Swiss Alps as watchdogs, pack animals, and trail breakers. They were then known as Alpine Mastiffs, and were invariably smooth-haired and, though large, were a great deal more active and less weighty than today's dog. By 1830 the breed was low in numbers and Newfoundlands were crossed in to give more strength. A legacy from this is the rough-coated dog.

The **Leonberger** was created by Herr Essig of
Leonberg when, in 1855, he tried to produce a dog to
look like the lions on the coat of arms of the German
town. He was an animal lover and a great showman
who owned both St. Bernards and Newfoundlands,
and he crossed these and then inbred for several
generations. Establishing breed types was extremely
difficult and it was not until 1949 that an official
standard was published by the Federation Cynologique
Internationale. The color is preferably yellow, or
golden like a lion, with a black mask on the face. The
minimum height is supposed to be 30in. This dog
should have a lively temperament as well as size and
substance. This has always been a fairly localized
breed and its numbers have been badly hit by the two
World Wars.

The **Tibetan Mastiff** is referred to in nearly all the breed histories of large dogs as the source from which their size and substance were derived. No direct evidence ever seems to be produced for this statement, nor is there much to connect the few Tibetan Mastiffs around today with the "mastiff dogs as big as asses" described by Marco Polo. The few Tibetan Mastiffs that there are live in America. They are one of the smaller of the giant breeds with a wide height range of 22 to 27in. They are heavily boned, deliberate in their movement, and have an expression both solomn and thoughtful. The coat is long and straight with a thick heavy undercoat and a mane across the shoulders. The thick and bushy tail is set on high and carried curled over the back. The color is black and tan or golden.

Tibetan Mastiff.

The **Great Dane** is misleadingly named, for it is a German breed called in its homeland the German Mastiff, or simply the German Dog. It is a breed which combines elegance with power to a remarkable degree. There is no mistaking the muscular strength nor the pride of bearing in the outline of a Dane. The movement should be lithe, springy, and free, attributes you would expect in a much smaller dog than one that weighs at least 120lb and is over 30in, in height. The head is always held high, the expression is alert, and the breed is required to have a look of dash and daring. The coat is short, sleek, and dense, and the majority of Danes are fawn in color, often with black masks. Brindle, blue (from light gray to deep slate), and black Danes are also correct, though quality is more difficult to achieve with the last two colors. The fifth color is without doubt the most striking. Called Harlequin, the background is

Great Dane Puppies

Great Dane

white with either black or blue patches, having the appearance of being ragged.

The Great Dane is found across the world. Its ears are cropped everywhere but in Britain, where the ears are required to be small and dropped. In the past the Great Dane was often called the German Boarhound, a name which tells us of its original use. Bred in large

163

numbers at the courts of the ducal German states, boarhounds probably came in all sorts of shapes and sizes, but by the 19th century the present type had emerged. The dog needs ample space to be seen at its best.

Mastiff dogs have been known to weigh more than 235lb; they and St. Bernards are the heaviest breeds. The minimum height should be 30in and substance should be in proportion. The dog should combine a look of grandeur with good nature and have courage combined with docility. It makes a quiet but very effective guard but needs human contact to make the most of its loyalty and character. The head should be large and square, and broad between the ears and across the muzzle, which should be blunt across the end. This broad deep muzzle is a feature of the mastiff group as a whole. The eyes are small and hazel brown. The ears are also small and set on the skull in such a way as to increase the impression of width. The legs are heavily boned, and the ribcage is both wide and deep, so that the girth is fully one third more than the height at the shoulder. The hindquarters are equally broad and muscular, finished off by a thick rooted long tail. The coat is short and close-lying and the color can be apricot. silver, fawn or brindle. The muzzle, ears, and nose should be black.

Breeding and rearing so large a dog, for maximum substance without losing soundness, is a formidable challenge to breeders. All the giant breeds suffer

Mastiff

during times when money or food is short, and the Mastiff underwent a great set back during the Second World War. There were not enough animals left to form a breeding nucleus, and stock from America and Canada had to be imported to ensure that what is considered a traditional English breed did not die out. The word mastiff occurs throughout historical times referring to large dogs, particularly of the guarding type Bas reliefs show the broad-muzzled mastiff type existed in Assyria by about 700 B.C. When the Romans invaded Britain, they found a mastiff type so big and so ferocious, that such dogs were sent to Rome for wild beast fights.

165

Neopolitan Mastiff

The **Neopolitan Mastiff** is Italy's representative in
the mastiff group. The dog has the required broad
muzzle and the heavy dewlaps, which distinguish the
type and height of 28in and a weight of 150lb. The
color should be black or leaden gray and the coat is
short and fine. The skin in supple and abundant,
particularly on the massive, monolithic head, which
has the appearance of being covered with
overstretched baggy velvet. Traditionally, these dogs
wear a very broad, heavily studded collar, fringed on
the edges with badger hair. The dog has the broad
deep body common to all mastiffs and the tail, docked
to two-thirds, is particularly thick and blunt. This dog
has a strong guarding instinct.

The **Shar Pei** originally came from southern China, where it was used as a fighting dog. The height is about 20in and the dog has the straight hind legs, the stilted action, and the blue-black tongue of that other Chinese breed, the Chow. Since the Chow has a smooth coat version, it is possible that the two breeds have something in common. The Shar Pei is remarkable for its very wrinkled skin. The coat is short, very bristly, and hard, and this, together with the loose skin, is supposed to give the dog a protective advantage when fighting. The color can be black or any shade of brown through cream. The Shar Pei has a short, compact body and a very broad, blunt muzzle. Like many dogs bred for fighting the Shar Pei has a clam and friendly temperament toward the human race. Unfortunately the wrinkled head predisposes the breed to eye troubles.

Shar Pei

167

Bull Breeds

The **Bulldog** is considered a symbol of courage and tenacity, a legacy from its bloodthirsty past. The dog today is a thickset one, heavily boned, low on the leg and weighing about 55lb. It should be broad, powerful, and compact though it does not seem to

Bulldogs

Bulldog

present the active appearance called for by the standard. The head is massive, so much so that the dog looks top-heavy. The upturned jaw, the heavy flews, and the mass of wrinkles on the face have led to the affectionate title of sourpuss! The short, broad muzzle, the undershot mouth, and the deep underjaw mean that the nose is "laid back" or receding, confirmation that enables the Bulldog to hang on to a victim without suffocating. The body is broad, short, and thick, with the round deep chest slung between the widely spaced forelegs, an arrangement that gives the dog stability. The hindquarters are comparatively light, the Bulldog having all its weight up front. The tail. is naturally short, as is the smooth coat. Black or black an tan are inadmissible colors.

The Bulldog today is both amiable and obstinate. The battered heavyweight look has charm but the exaggerated shape tends to make this a short-lived breed, since they are prone to respiratory troubles and heart attacks. The bull-baiting dogs, from which the breed descended, were higher on the leg, lighter in build, and longer in muzzle.

169

The **Bull Mastiff** is a breed developed in the 19th century and recognized by the British Kennel Club in the 20th. However, before any attempt was made to breed this type of dog systematically, animals approaching the Bull Mastiff, both in size and appearance, were certainly used as guards. At the end of the 18th century George Morland painted this type of dog, and the French naturalist Buffon described something similar. The Bronte sisters wrote about their own dog as "black muzzled and tawny" and "of a breed between mastiff and bulldog" Obviously, this particular cross between the two breeds was fairly common and regarded as a successful way of getting a sizeable and active guard dog. The Victorians were very fond of the first cross produced by two distinct breeds. They made a lot of similar experiments between gundogs, and there is no reason to suppose that it was not also tried with guard dogs and, for that matter, toys.

One of the reasons for the establishment of the Bull Mastiff was the direct result of the very harsh game laws. Estate owners anxious to preserve their game birds and protect their shooting rights, were in a position to get legislation passed which made poaching a rabbit an offense for which the poacher could be transported. The running battles between gamekeepers and poachers became very rough and the gamekeepers enlisted the help of large, dark, silent dogs which were known as Keeper's Night Dogs. These were weighty animals who, even if securely muzzled, could knock down a running man and keep

Bull Mastiff

him pinned down until law and order arrived. Crossing Mastiffs with Bulldogs finally produced, in the hand of dedicated breeders, a stable type that bred true and the Bull Mastiff was recognized as a separate breed in 1924. The Bull Mastiff should show great strength, but not be cumbersome. Its height is about 27in and weight about 130lb. The short coat can be any shade of fawn, brindle, or red and a black muzzle is essential.

171

The **Boxer** is another breed which numbers the Bulldog among its ancestors. Boxers came from Germany, and the name is something of a mystery. This is even more suprising when we know that the Boxer is a comparatively modern breed, a product of the decade between 1890 and 1900. Germany has always had a particular interest in police, guard, and frontier patrol dogs and has developed and established a number of breeds for these purposes. The Boxer has many of the features that distinguish the mastiff group, including the broad muzzle and the undershot jaw, and is widely used in Europe as a service dog working with the police and the army. Very little known outside its homeland until after the Second World War, it then enjoyed an upsurge of popularity in both America and Britain. It was a particularly

Boxer

**Boxer
(cropped ears)**

successful show dog with great ring presence: statuesque, muscular, and yet with great personality.

This is a breed of vibrant energy, both boisterous and exuberant, and many novice owners in the breed's first wave of popularity found that they had taken on more than they had bargained for. However, properly taught, the Boxer makes a great family dog for the energetic. The height is about 24in and the weight about 66lb. The permissible colors are all shades of fawn and brindling with a dark muzzle which is almost obligatory in the mastiff group. White markings are almost essential for show dogs in America and Britain. They may include a white muzzle, white blaze up the forehead, and white chest and legs. European Boxers are often plainer, since such marking is considered to make them too conspicuous when they are working.

The **French Bulldog** is a breed that has been in existence for about 100 years. There were a number of attempts made to bantamize the Bulldog, but toy Bulldogs did not become established and the Frenchie did. The head is massive, square, and broad, with a short, flat muzzle and an undershot mouth. The ears are upright, wide at the base and set high on the head. The body is that of an active and robust animal, strongly boned and with a smooth lustrous coat. The ideal weight is about 28lb and the colors include brindle, pied, and fawn. Originating in France and now popular in Europe and America, these dogs have playful and friendly characters with a strong comfort-loving streak.

French Bulldog

The **Boston Terrier** is a product of America and is yet another offshoot from the original Bulldog rootstock. The breed was created in and around Boston by a number of people who were interested in fighting dogs and therefore bull breeds in general. Included in the Boston's ancestry are the Bulldog, One of the smooth-coated terriers, and probably the Frenchie. The result is a very smart little dog, recognized in its homeland in three weight divisions (lightweight, under 15lb, middleweight, 15-20lb, heavyweight 20-25lb) but being generally about 18lb in Europe. The dog should be either brindle and white or black and white, with the placing of the white markings considered particularly important.

Boston Terriers

175

The **Bull Terrier** standard states that it is the gladiator of the canine race, and for this reason sets no weight and height limits, merely remarking that there should be the maximum of substance to the size of the dog. The breed was originally developed for the so-called sport of dog fighting, which flourished as a betting sport through much of the 19th century. The Bulldog, developed for bull-baiting, was too slow and cumbersome to be successful fighting in the dog pits. Thus terriers, in particular the Old English White, were crossed in to give speed and agility without sacrificing the courage or tenacity necessary for a fighting dog. The all-white Bull Terrier owes its origin to a Mr. Hinks of Birmingham, England who, in the early 1860s, took the rather short-faced brindle bull and terriers common at the time and crossed in the Old English White Terrier, a breed now extinct. The resulting more elegant and agile white animal was derided by the fanciers of the older type, until Mr.

Bull terrier (white)

Bull terrier (colored)

176

Hink's bitch Puss defeated her opponent in a sponsored fight one day and won a prize at a dog show the next. Both colored and all-white Bull Terriers are shown now, and in Britain there is also a Miniature Bull Terrier recognized at under 14in. The head of the Bull Terrier is one of its most striking features, being egg-shaped with a gently curving profile and no hollows or indentations. The eye is small, triangular, and obliquely placed. In the days of the fighting dog the ears were cropped, but after the British Kennel Club banned cropping in 1895 breeders developed a dog in which the ears were naturally small, neat, and erect.

Bull terriers are strong, boisterous, and make good-natured family dogs who are easy going with children but often intolerant and aggressive with other animals.

Miniature Bull Terrier

The **Staffordshire Bull Terrier** was not recognized as a pedigree animal until 1935. Part of this was due to a wide divergence in type and appearance and part possibly to the dog's unsavory past. These too were dogs bred for fighting, in which courage and gameness were counted the supreme virtues and money could be made by betting on them. Like many fighting breeds, today's Staffordshire is a dog both confident and kindly toward the human race, but often a troublemaker with other dogs.

Staffordshire Bull Terrier

**American Pit
Bull Terrier**

The **American Pit Bull Terrier** is the fighting dog
of the States. This dog has much the same fighting
ancestry as the Staffordshire Bull Terrier but has been
developed into a larger animal, 19in in height instead
of 16in, and some 46lb instead of about 35lb. In
selecting the characteristics to produce a breed of dog
which fights without quarter, man has gone for
dominant animals with a high pain threshold. If you
want to keep one dog only and you live in an isolated
area, Pit Bull Terriers make good guards. They are
extremely strong dogs for their size and have a
suprising quickness and grace for such a heavily built
animal.

Shepherd and Guard Breeds

The **Pinscher** is one of the rarities in the Pinscher/Schnauzer group of breeds, all of which originated in Germany. Historically, the Pinscher and Schnauzers are deemed to have shared the same background, though it is a very long while since both the coarse- and smooth-haired puppies occurred in the same litter. The Pinscher, sometimes known as the Middle Pinscher, is one size up from the Miniature Pinscher, its better known relative, and stands about 16½in at the shoulder. This is rather a squarely build dog with a sober appearance, looking robust and well muscled.

Pinscher

Doberman

The **Doberman** is also included in the Pinscher/Schnauzer group in Germany, though, historically, it is a very modern breed. It is the creation of a single man, Herr Dobermann, who worked in the 1870s to produce a guard dog *par excellence*. Very agile, fast, quick-thinking, and both powerful and elegant, Dobermans have been widely used throughout the world as police, service, and security dogs. Their creator wanted a tough, sharp breed, and they still need careful handling and training if they are not to become anti-social nuisances. The ideal height is about 27in and black, brown, blue, or fawn, all with tan markings, are the acceptable colors.

181

The **Giant** or **Riesenschnauzer**, the largest and least popular of the Schnauzers, is a dog from Bavaria, where it has been used in the past for droving both cattle and pigs; droving is the movement of livestock on foot over considerable distances. As with many droving dogs, it would have died out when its use declined, but it was recognized in Germany as a useful police and service dog. The size is about 25½in and Giant Schnauzers are often black, though salt and pepper (showing various shades of gray) is acceptable.

The **Standard Schnauzer** was the first to make an impact outside its German homeland, reaching both

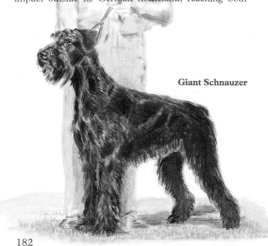

Giant Schnauzer

Standard Schnauzer

America and Britain in the 1920s. Like all of the Schnauzers, the Standard is a squarely built dog, robust and sinewy. It should have an air of reliability and appear a dog of both strength and vigor. This is probably the oldest of the three breeds, going back four centuries or so.

The most popular of the Schnauzers today is the **Miniature Schnauzer** which should be about 14in in height, about 5in less than its Standard relative. Both these breeds were renowned as ratters and are considered terriers in America and Canada, where they are among the most popular in the group. As with many terriers, the coats of all the

183

**Miniature
Schnauzers**

Schnauzers need a lot of stripping and trimming. Salt and pepper is the usual color.

The **Tibetan Terrier** is one of a number of breeds, developed and exhibited in the western world, believed to have come from that remote and mountainous country. The word development is crucial, as at the turn of the century the differences between Tibetan Terriers, Lhasa Apso, and even Shih Tzus were not discernible to outside observers. The two larger breeds were often lumped together under the name Lhasa Terrier. However, by the 1930s, the Tibetan Terrier was recognized as a purebred animal in Britain, (it was not imported into the United States until 1956 and the AKC did not take over the registration of the breed until 1973) though it is not a terrier in any sense, and is regarded as a herding dog in its native land. There it was a rural dog, a watchdog, one that traveled with the merchant's caravans, or guarded the nomadic herdsman's animals and possessions. It is fairly small as herding dogs go - about 16in – but it should be well muscled, active and game. The standard suggest that it should look not unlike an Old English Sheepdog in miniature. Certainly it has the same compact and powerful body, but the Tibetan Terrier has a natural undocked tail, which is carried in a curl over the back. The coat should be double, with a fine wool undercoat and a long, profuse, fine top coat which should be straight or very slightly waved. In Tibet the dog was shorn in the summer and its hair used for weaving. Color was therefore considered important, with pure black or pure white being prized. It is believed to be the only breed in the world that is required to have large, flat feet.

Tibetan Terrier

The **Lhasa Apso** is another watchdog that comes from Tibet. This dog was a guardian of the town houses, monasteries, and palaces, a small "barking sentinel" to warn of strangers within the gates. Such dogs were often believed to have religious significance and were treated with great respect, and this awe made them even more effective as watchdogs. In shape the Apso is a well–balanced, compact little dog, longer in body than it is high – 10in. It is very heavily coated with a straight, hard top coat to floor level and a soft, woolly undercoat. The tail is well feathered and carried right over the back; it often has a kink at the end. Preferred colors are gold and honey, but all shades and multicolors are acceptable.

Lhasa Apso

Bernese Mountain Dog

The **Bernese Mountain Dog** is one of four separate breeds from the Swiss cantons. All four breeds are closely related and were used as cattle dogs and droving animals. The Bernese, which is one of the two biggest of the group, was also used as a draft animal, pulling small carts. The dog is a strong, sturdy working animal, rather above medium size – 27in. Bernese Mountain Dogs are slow to mature but respond well to training and the standard stresses that they should be good–natured, self-confident, and friendly. Their coat is soft and silky, with a bright, natural sheen. The color is always jet black, set off with rich reddish brown markings, a white blaze on the head, and a white shirtfront.

187

Puli

The **Puli** is a shepherd dog of the Hungarian plains, an agile, nimble, and active dog about 17½in, in height and about 33lb in weight. The most remarkable thing about the Puli is its coat. It is known almost invariably outside Hungary as an exhibitor's dog, since a properly presented Puli is a fascinating sight. The coat, which in some cases grows to floor length, falls naturally into the desired narrow cords as soon as the dog matures. The dog in many ways gives the impression of being densely covered with lengths of frayed string, so densely covered in fact, that it is sometimes difficult to tell one end from the other. The usual color is black, often weathered or rusty and faded in tone.

The **Komondor** is one of a number of large white guarding breeds spread across Europe. This breed is one of the two Hungarian versions and is a massive 31in. It is an impressive dog, made even more so by the wealth of corded coat. The hair is extremely profuse and long, with a cottony texture that causes it to felt and mat easily. It can, however, be encouraged to cord, and most Komondors are shown with the coat hanging like tassels. The dog will not be fully coated until it is two or more, at which stage the coat will be an impenetrable mass. This effectively protects the dog against any sort of attack and any sort of weather conditions but poses problems of hygiene for the owner. The Komondor possesses a very strong guarding instinct and is not a dog for a novice.

Komondor

189

The **German Shepherd Dog** is not a very old breed in comparison with some, yet, in numerical terms, it is probably the most popular dog in the world. The credit for the temperamental and physical characteristics which make it the most versatile of working dogs must go to the German fanciers who established the breed some 90 years ago. Sheepdogs from the areas of Wurttemburg and Thuringia provided the basis. Such dogs were used, not only to protect sheep, but also to prevent the flocks from straying from the pasture on to the unfenced arable land. These were dogs that had to be constantly watchful, virtually tireless, and able to act on their own initiative. It is very much a combination of these same qualities that accounts for the success of the modern German Shepherd as a working dog. This is a strong and agile animal with an effortless, springy gait which lets the dog cover the ground with easy, natural energy-saving strides. Height should be about 26in and color is not considered important, but white is not allowed nor are the very heavy fluffy coats that appear on some specimens. The coat should be double with the harsh outer coat being up to 2in in length, very dense, and weather resistant. This is a dog that works well in any climate, for this type of coat acts as an insulator for extremes of both heat and cold.

German breeders have always recognized that temperament is of equal importance to conformation in a working dog. The combination which makes the German Shepherd so formidable is alertness,

German Shepherd Dog

reliability, and the power of concentration. The willingness and the determination of the German Shepherd has made the breed the premier choice of police forces and all other organizations that need to use reliable trained dogs in quantity. Stamina, agility, the ability to concentrate, plus the desire to please its trainer, are some of the essentials needed in a breed that fulfils so many roles, from guiding the blind to locating avalanche victims. The German Shepherd was unknown outside Germany before the First World War, when their use on the battlefields, as messenger dogs and as rescue dogs locating the wounded, brought them to the attention of both American and British soldiers.

191

Tervueren

Belgian Shepherd Dogs comprise four distinct breeds, though only one has achieved wide recognition outside its homeland. These breeds all belong to a group of similar European Herding dogs of which the best known is the German Shepherd and the least known the dutch Shepherd dogs. The varieties of Belgian Shepherd differ only in coat and color. They are, compared with German shepherds,

192

rather lightlybuilt, slender dogs, shorter in the back and higher on the leg. The ears are erect and the tail is carried low. All the Belgian Shepherd Dogs have a distinctive high head carriage and an alert and attentive look. They are wary of strangers, being natural guards, and make good obedience and agility dogs. The height of all for breeds can be up to 26in.

The **Groenendael** is the one best known in both America and Britain. It has a long, straight black coat of medium harshness with a dense undercoat, for it is emphasised that these dogs should be able to withstand adverse weather conditions.

The **Tevueren** also has a long, straight, and abundant coat, but the colors include all shades of red, fawn, and gray. Characteristically each hair has a blackened tip, so the mature Tevueren has a shaded coat which may be particularly dark on the shoulders and back. The facial mask is black.

The **Malinois** is short-coated, but with the same black overlay on a reddish mahogany coat.

The **Laekenois**, rarest of the four, has a coat described as rough, dry, and untidy looking.

Top: **Malinois**
Middle: **Laekenois**
Bottom: **Groenendael**

193

The **Briard** or **Berger de Brie** is one of the guard cum shepherd dogs which were and integral part of rural life when large predators and sheep thieves were both more common than they are today. The Briard does not seem to have been confined to the province of France from which it takes its name, but was in use over a much wider area. It is a strong, muscular dog up to 27in at the withers, a dog of rugged appearance, which should also look well proportioned and supple. The head is large and rectangular with a big, black, square nose. The eyes are large and dark brown, gentle, even humorous, in expression. Ears are often cropped in Europe but are drop in Britain. Both cropped and drop ears are accepted in the United States. The neck and body are muscular with the back firm and level. The body is very slightly longer than the dog is high. Movement should be effortless, covering a great deal of ground, the dog being built to turn quickly as well as move fast. The hindlegs have double dewclaws set low on the back pasterns, and these are considered of great importance. The tail is long, carried low, and has an upward hook at the tip. The coat is long, not less than 3in on the body, and is slightly wavy and very dry to the touch. It has been likened to goat hair, but goats do not have the fine, dense undercoat required of the Briard. Colors include black and the darker shades of fawn, sometimes with a black overlay and shading.

Young Briards are lively and high–spirited dogs who find it difficult to concentrate long enough to be taught easily. Like other slow-maturing breeds, however, once a lesson is learned it is retained forever.

Briard

Adult dogs have a serious attitude toward guarding their master's or mistress's property.

Breed type in the Briard seems to have remained fairly constant for some centuries. A breed club was founded in France about 1900. The First World War saw Briards used as pack dogs, carrying ammunition, as draft dogs, pulling light machine guns, and as Red Cross dogs, searching for the wounded. The Briard was taken home by American troops but did not reach Britain until the late 1960s.

The **Old English Sheepdog** is one of the family of shaggy sheepdogs that spread right across Europe, from Italy in the south to Russia in the north, and from Hungary in the east to Britain in the west. The Old English Sheepdog is a strong, compact-looking animal, thick set and symmetrical. The skull and muzzle are square and capacious and the nose is always black and large. This is one of the few breeds where walleyes (with a blue iris) are acceptable. Either one or both eyes may be like this, or they can be brown. There is no difference in the vision because of their color. The body is compact, with a deep and ample ribcage, and the dog is heavily boned for its size. Curiously, the dog's backline should be lower at the shoulder than at the loin and exhibitors do a lot of back-combing over the dog's rump to get this effect. The tail is always docked extremely short, and it is from this that the breed gets its nickname of Bobtail. The coat should be profuse and of hard texture, shaggy but not curly. The color can be any shade of gray, or blue, with or without white markings. In coat, color, and size the show Bobtail has altered a great deal during this century. The coat has gotten more profuse and softer in texture which, as far as the layman is concerned, means that grooming has now become almost unmanageable. The dog has also gotten much bigger and heavier, for the standard gives a minimum size of only 22in and most Bobtails are nearer 27in. The dog has an ambling gait at slow speeds which makes it look deceptively clumsy. It is therefore something of a shock to see the Bobtail's elastic gallop and ability to swerve and turn while at full stretch. The bark has a loud and resonant ring to it. The Old English Sheepdog is a very popular breed today.

Old English Sheepdog

197

The **Bearded Collie** is another British member of
the European family of shaggy sheepdogs. The
Beardie is traditionally associated with Scotland,
where it was much used as a cattle and droving dog.
Droving is the movement of livestock on foot over
considerable distances. To control the semi-wild
herds, drovers needed strong, agile, and determined
dogs who could be trusted to look after their masters'
herds in all circumstances. The Beardie was also used
as a hill-gathering sheepdog, a fast and noisy dog sent
out in vast sweeps across moorland to gather the
scattered flocks and bring them back to the shepherd.

The Bearded Collie should be an alert, lively, self-
confident dog, with a lean and active appearance.

Bearded Collies

The face should have a bright, curious expression, with eyebrows that are arched up and forward over eyes whose color should match the coat color. The body is longer than it is high and the dog should be well boned and muscular. The movement should be supple and far reaching with the long tail carried low and only extended at speed. Height is about 22in and the long, shaggy harsh coat should be totally weatherproof. All shades of gray and brown are acceptable, with or without white markings. The Beardie is a fun-loving and bouncy dog that never seems to grow middle-aged or sedate. It makes a good family pet for the energetic.

The **Border Collie** is one of the world's finest working sheepdogs. Sheep farming in many areas would not be economical without dogs to gather, drive, select out, and pen the flocks. The term Border Collie became current about the turn of the century, but nimble black and white farm dogs bred to work have been portrayed since the 11th century, and probably existed long before that. Sheepdog Trials at the end of the 19th century enabled shepherds to test their dogs' skill. The first winners came from the Border country between Scotland and England and so a name was coined for what before had been called merely a sheepdog.

To gather sheep scattered on a mountainside a dog may need to run 40 or 50 miles in a day's work. Such a dog must have enormous stamina and tremendous drive to work. This energy and keenness makes the true working dog unsuitable as a pet, since inactivity will make such an animal frustrated and miserable. Many Borders are used in competitive obedience and agility tests, for they are lithe, fast, and quick to learn.

The breed has been shown for many years in Australia and has recently reached the show ring in Britain. The breed is accepted for registration by the UKC but not the AKC. It is therefore not shown at shows run by the AKC. The show dog is more uniform in appearance than the worker, heavier in coat, sturdier in bone, and rather more placid in temperament. Smooth coats as well as moderately long are acceptable, but rarely seen. Color is unspecified but white should not predominate. Height is about 21in.

Border Collies

The **Rough Collie** has been developed by 100 years of selective breeding from a working collie type that was very similar to the working collie of today. Indeed, the Rough Collie illustrates very well what can happen to a functional dog when it becomes an exhibition and companion animal. For one thing the breed becomes much more uniform in type, as appearance becomes the criterion. A lot of the drive, keenness, energy, and stamina needed by a working dog is blunted or lost. The coat becomes more profuse and magnificent, often losing its weather-

Rough Collie

proof and easy care qualities in the process. The Rough Collie was one of the first breeds to be developed like this for the show ring and has remained a popular dog. It is often called the Lassie dog, after the movie dog, and any breed with an almost universal nickname must be popular on both sides of the Atlantic. Rough Collies are about 24in high and weigh about 64lb. There are three recognized coat colors, all usually with white markings; sable (golden shades), tricolor or blue merle (clear, silvery blue marbled with black).

The **Smooth Collie** has a descriptive title for it is the only collie breed without a long coat. Possibly for this

Smooth Collie

reason it has never attracted the attention given to the other collie breeds and has always remained the favorite of just a few. The dog should be a replica of the Rough Collie, the same shape, the same size, the same colors. The only difference is in the short, flat, harsh topcoat. The latter, alas makes the dog look rather plain and angular compared with the Rough. Both breeds originated in the same area of Scotland and a century ago both types appeared in the same litters and were shown in the same classes.

The **Shetland Sheepdog** of today is a miniature of the show Rough Collie and, as such, is a particularly attractive and intelligent companion of a size suitable

Shetland Sheepdog

for both urban and rural life. The breed in its present form is of a fairly recent origin, being known as a show dog for little more than 70 years. The original sheepdog of the Shetland Isles had played an important role in the economy of the islands for centuries, but we have little by way of description of these early dogs except that they were often speckled, foxy-faced, and small in size. The fact that all the domestic animals of the Shetlands tend to be dwarfed compared with their mainland counterparts is probably due to the subsistence level of life there, which tended to favor the smaller individuals, and to the population isolation which led to inbreeding, also tending to diminish size. Early dogs were very plain little animals, looking far more like tiny working sheepdogs than the miniature Rough Collie that the Sheltie resembles today. Today's breed is exceptionally gentle, sweet-natured, and sensitive with the corollary that some individuals lack confidence. Much of their visual charm lies in the profuse coat with its abundant mane and frill. Size is about 14 ½in.

The **Bouvier des Flandres** was a cattle-droving dog and a general–purpose farm worker. Dogs can be 27in in height and 88lb weight, and the breed looks a dog of great strength with a sturdy body set on rather short, strong legs. The tail is docked short, which adds to the square, heavyweight impression. The hair is course and dry to the touch, about 2½in long and unkempt looking. This harsh, crinkly topcoat is usually dark in color, often brindled or shaded, and covers a dense fine undercoat. The head appears big because of the dog's beard, moustache, and beetling eyebrows, which all help to give a rather surly and forbidding expression. However, though this is a formidable guard dog if roused, the temperament in normal circumstances is calm and sensible.

The **Maremma** is one of the two Italian herding breeds beginning to be known outside their homeland. Large, all-white, and with a bear-like head, it is a working guard dog found in the Abruzzi area of central Italy, where it is very much an outdoor type

Bouvier des Flandres

Maremma

animal, having a long rather harsh coat forming a ruff around the neck and being completely weather-proof. The breed is a very hardy one and in the worst of weather conditions still manages to look clean and white. There are a number of large, white guarding breeds in Europe, including the Great Pyrenées Dog and the Hungarian Kuvasz. It is possible that all share a common ancestor in some dog which the Magyars brought with them in their western migration. White was the preferred color so that shepherds could distinguish them easily from the main predator, the wolf, and so that the sheep accepted their presence more calmly.

The **Rottweiler** is described as a stalwart dog of above average size. The appearance is that of a strong, active heavyweight with males up to 27in in height and weighing as much as 120lb. Despite their size, there is nothing slack or cumbersome about either the looks or the movement of a good Rottweiler. The dog's very compactness suggests latent power. This is a guard dog, much used for police and army work, and its bearing should display boldness and courage. The dark brown eyes should look out tranquilly on the world suggesting an inherent good nature. The keen, suspicious gaze, habitual with some guarding breeds, is foreign to the Rottweiler until its attention is aroused by something untoward. The head is broad, with a deep, strong muzzle, a large black nose, and small drop ears. The neck is very strong and muscular. It is thick and round in cross section, as is the body with its roomy deep rib cage. Both fore- and hindquarters are very muscular and strongly boned. The tail is cut off to leave a stump, which is carried horizontally. The coat is double, as it should be with all working dogs, with the outer coat being coarse and flat. The color is always black, with clearly defined markings which can vary from rich tan to mahogany brown.

The Rottweiler is a breed with a long history. It takes its name from the town of Rottweil in West Germany where it was known for some centuries as a droving or cattle dog and had the alternative name of the Rottweil Butchers' Dog. Such animals may have reached Germany in the first place with the Roman

Rottweiler

invaders, for such armies took their food with them in the shape of herds of cattle. The Swiss Mountain Dog breeds bear a familial likeness to the Rottweiler and may be part of a chain of droving dogs left behind as the Romans crossed the Alps and marched northward. Such dogs formed the basis for a number of breeds and were subsequently used for a number of different purposes. Rottweil was a market town for a large cattle-raising area, so Rottweilers remained cattle dogs, often carrying the cattle dealers' purses strung around their necks as they escorted their masters' purchases home. The breed was saved from extinction by the realization that it was excellent for police work.

Corgis were also cattle dogs and belong to a group of herding dogs often referred to as heelers. These dogs should be nimble, active, and strong, have fairly long bodies and rather short legs. Their job was to fly in and nip the heels of the bullocks, dodging the retaliatory kicks which whistled harmlessly over their heads. There are two breeds of Corgi, both of which come from Wales. The name is believed to come from the Welsh *cor*, meaning to gather together, and *gi*, which is dog. Both the Cardigan and the Pembroke Welsh Corgi come from South Wales, yet each is a very distinct breed in its own right, illustrating the inaccessibility of the Welsh valleys.

The **Pembroke Corgi** is the better known of the two breeds and is very popular as a pet and show dog.

Welsh Corgi Cardigan

Its 60 years in the show ring have altered the Pembroke: it is a heavier and much more cloddy dog than it was and would no longer be active enough for its original function. However, it still retains the wit to assess a situation, the intelligence to make the best use of it, the noisy bark, and the occasional desire to rush in and nip something, all attributes from its heeling past. The usual colors are red, or black and tan, with white markings. The height is about 12in and the weight often as much as 24lb.

The **Cardigan Corgi** has remained relatively unchanged. It has a long, fox's brush of a tail and large upright ears. This is a quieter and more placid dog than the Pembroke and comes in a wider variety of colors, including blue merle.

Welsh Corgi Pembroke

The **Valhund** is a Swedish heeling dog. Again this was a general-purpose farm dog, kept for shifting the animals, warning of the approach of strangers, and catching rats in the hay and straw barns. The dog was commonly used and little regarded, and it was not until the late 1940s that it was suddenly realized that the breed was in grave danger of disappearing. The Swedish Kennel Club gave it official recognition and some dedicated breeders started to popularize it, both as a show and companion animal. The Valhund should be a small, powerful, low to ground dog, and resembles in shape the old style Pembroke Corgi, being higher on the leg – 13in – and lighter in build than the modern Pembroke. The impression one gets is of a watchful, alert, and energetic working dog.

Valhund

Lancashire Heeler

The **Lancashire Heeler** was used in the district around Ormskirk, in the county of Lancashire, in England by butchers and slaughterhousemen to control and direct the beasts to be killed. The dogs were often affectionately known as "nip 'n duck" dogs because that was their style of working. They show a strong terrier influence, especially in the head qualities, and have some of the same enthusiasm, both in their attitude to herding cattle and in their keenness to hunt rats. The height at the shoulders should be about 12in and the body length should be just a little longer than the height. The tail is set high and carried gaily over the back when the dog is excited. The smooth, glossy coat should be black with rich tan markings.

Australian Cattle Dog

The **Australian Cattle Dog** is one of the world's toughest working dogs with regard to stamina. Many dogs that are successful in the working sphere are hard both in body and mind. Cattle dogs do not adapt easily to a quiet life with nothing to do and should only be kept by those who can give them an energetic and active life. Inactivity can sour the temperament of the more vigorous breeds, and Cattle Dogs, noted for their endurance and hardiness, need some form of training and work that occupies their potentials. In Australia these dogs control vast herds of cattle, both on open grazing lands and in the close quarters of the stockyards. They are adaptable enough to work in near tropical heat. The smooth coat is about 1in in length and two color schemes are approved, either blue-mottled or red-speckled.

The **Anatolian Shepherd Dog** is another of the large guarding breeds used by shepherds all across Europe and Asia. These dogs are not expected to control the flocks, which are often led by the shepherd rather than driven, but are expected to protect them, especially against wolves. The breed probably belongs to the mastiff group, for they are large dogs with stamina and speed, and they have the broad head which distinguishes this family. The coat is dense and smooth, usually fawn with a black mask, but a white version is also recognized. The height can be 32in and the weight 145lb. This breed is totally unsuited to town life and is not for the novice owner.

**Anatolian
Shepherd Dog**

Terriers

The **Airedale Terrier**, the biggest terrier and named after the Yorkshire valley, in England are keen of expression, quick of movement, and easily excited by the unfamiliar or the unexpected. The eyes are dark and small, set in a long, flat skull with a powerful muzzle and neat drop

Airedale Terrier

Glen of Imaal Terrier

ears. Dogs can be up to 24in in height, making them a useful size for police and guard work, for which they are used in Europe. The coat should be hard, dense, and wiry, and not so long as to appear ragged, something that cannot be achieved without time-consuming trimming. The body color is black or dark gray, with legs and head tan. The tail is docked about half way.

The **Glen of Imaal Terrier** comes from the glen of that name in County Wicklow, Ireland. A small working terrier, it was bred as a fighting dog, a pursuit that seems to come naturally to most of Ireland's terriers. It was used also to go to ground after such animals as badgers. Height is about 14in and weight about 35lb. The head appears large for so small a dog and the front legs are slightly bowed. The coat is longish and untrimmed and the colors include

Bedlington Terrier

blue, blue and tan and wheaten. The tail is docked to a medium length.

The **Bedlington Terrier** is a dog of graceful, flowing curves, contrasting sharply with the straight-edged silhouette of most of the terriers. The Bedlington is capable of some speed. The breed, or the beginnings of it, existed some 200 years ago, when they were valued for their gameness and their rabbit-catching abilities. They did not have the exaggerated lamb-like look of today's show stock, but the arched loins and racy hind-quarters were already in evidence. Dogs should be about 16in and 23lb in weight. The lamb-like clip should not deceive you, for when roused the Bedlington is courageous and full of temper.

The **Manchester Terrier** is one of the few smooth-coated terrier breeds. By the end of the 18th century, terriers were roughly divided by size (long vs. short legs), coat (smooth vs. wire and color (white vs. black and tan). The Manchester was the smooth-coated, long-legged, black and tan. It was then simply called the Black and Tan, and there was a wire-haired version as well, which became extinct, leaving only traces of its influence in the ancestry of breeds such as the Airedale. The name Manchester Terrier only became current in the 1920s, though the breed is one of the oldest terrier types. It is an alert dog, easy to care for, and a compact size, being some about 16in in height. It has never been very popular, possibly because it seems to lack personality.

Manchester Terrier

The **Border Terrier** is one of the less artificially presented terrier breeds. The tail is a natural length and the harsh coat may be tidied for the exhibition dog but otherwise requires only normal brushing. Borders were hunt terriers, coming from the Border country between England and Scotland. They had to be small enough to go to ground after a fox and large enough to keep up with a horse, and weighed about 16lb. They are both quieter and less aggressive than many terriers. Colors include red, wheaten, and gray.

Border Terriers

**Lakeland
Terrier**

The **Lakeland Terrier** is another of the hunt terriers of the north of England. In a sheep-rearing area foxes are pests, and terriers, such as the Lakeland, were expected to follow the fox underground and force it out into the open for the waiting hounds. Each district had its own name for the terriers who did this job, among which were the Cumberland, the Patterdale, and the Fell Terrier. In 1923 an association was formed to look after these terriers' interests and the definitive name of Lakeland was chosen. The breed was refined and standardized. They became shorter in the leg and rather heavier. Today's dog presents a very barbered appearance. They are usually gray or black with faded tan on the legs and head. Height should be about 14½in and weight about 17lb.

221

The **Fox Terrier (Smooth)** and the **Fox Terrier (Wire)** are considered two different breeds, though their origin and purpose in life were the same: to bolt the fox from its earth to the waiting hounds. Since they were expected to travel with the foxhound pack, these terriers had to have both speed and endurance. They needed strength and courage to face an opponent, as well equipped as they were, in the narrow confines of an underground lair. Many of the early huntsmen preferred their hunt terriers to be predominantly white, since this minimized the chances of the dog being mistaken for the prey in the heat of the moment. Though they have left their working past far behind, Fox Terriers are still mainly white in color, with either black or tan patches. The Smooth Fox Terrier was a popular dog in the early part of this century but was overtaken by the Wire, which became the top favorite in the 1930s, since when both breeds have declined in numbers.

The coat of the Smooth is flat and hard in texture, easy to keep clean, and to groom. The coat of the Wire Fox Terrier is coarse and crinkly in texture with a soft, woolly undercoat. This coat has to be kept trimmed if the dog is to present the expected attractive, clean-cut appearance. Both breeds are alert and enthusiastic. Unless carefully handled some Fox Terriers can be over excitable, noisy, and aggressive to other dogs. The height for both breeds should be about 15½in and the weight 18lb.

Smooth-haired Fox Terrier

Wire-haired Fox Terrier

The **Norwich Terriers** come from the same root and in America are all known under the former title, as they were in Britain until 1964. Because the breeders of the prick-eared dogs could not agree with those of the drop-eared variety, the British Kennel Club allowed them to separate into two breeds, with the drop-eared type assuming the name of Norfolk Terrier. They are England's only short-legged terrier, and are amongst the smallest of the terrier tribe, being under 10in at the shoulder. They are busy, energetic little dogs, constitutionally hardy, like most of the terriers, and pleasant and fearless in temperament. Unlike many terriers, they are not particularly quarrelsome. They should look compact and strong, with plenty of substance and bone. The muzzle is wedge-shaped and the skull wide. The ears, whether erect or dropped, should be of medium size and

**Norwich Terrier
(drop-eared)**

**Norwich Terrier
(prick-eared)**

the eyes are small and dark with a bright expression. Like most terriers, they have strong, large teeth to enable them to enable them to bite, shake and kill their prey. The coat is hard, straight, and wiry, lying flat to the body but with a thick undercoat. The hair on the head is short and smooth except for whiskers and eyebrows. That on the neck and shoulders is longer and rougher, almost forming a mane. Colors include all shades of red, red wheaton, black and tan, or gray. In practice the deep reds are the most favored by breeders. White marks are unacceptable. These terriers originated in East Anglia, England, where a small red type of "earth" dog has been the preferred mouse catcher since at least the beginning of the 19th century.

The **Welsh Terrier** is one of two terrier breeds originating in Wales. Like the Lakeland Terrier which it resembles quite closely, the Welsh was probably an offshoot of the old rough-haired Black and Tan Terrier. Such dogs were used as hunt terriers, particularly in North Wales, where they ran with the hounds in pursuit of hill foxes. The Welsh Terrier was introduced to the show ring 100 years ago or so, making it one of the oldest show terrier breeds, and the type has been known since the end of the 18th century. Since their ancestors were kennelled with the hound pack, the Welsh had to learn to tolerate other dogs and is therefore not very quarrelsome. The color is black and bright tan. The size is about 15½in and 21lb.

Welsh Terrier

Irish Terrier

There is little but speculation as to how and when the first recognizable **Irish Terrier** was bred. The Dublin show of 1874 had classes for the Irish type but, as these were divided into those over and those under 9lb, the entrants cannot have resembled today's dog, which should be about 27lb in weight and 18in in height. These proportions make this one of the most streamlined of the terriers. The breed is a whole-colored one, usually a bright red, and the hard, wiry coat requires a great deal of trimming to achieve the required show presentation. The character of the Irish Terrier combines extreme sweetness toward its owners with an equally fiery attitude to other dogs, hence the breed's nickname: "the Dare Devil."

Kerry Blue Terrier

The Kerry Blue Terrier comes from the south and the western provinces of Ireland. It was not recognized as a pedigree animal until the 1920s, but had obviously been a purebred type for a considerable length of time before then. Early Kerries were kept as working farm dogs, herding sheep and cattle, ratting, and going to ground after fox and badger. They are dogs that like water, and it is even claimed that you can train a Kerry to retrieve. Kerry Blues have a soft, silky coat, plentiful and very wavy. They were originally shown in the rough, but are now a very much sculpted and trimmed breed, with a well-scissored outline. Kerry puppies are born black and lighten to the required blue shade at about a year old. The height is about 19in and the weight 37lb.

The **Soft-coated Wheaten Terrier** is another terrier with a soft, silky coat, which can be loosely waved or curled. The coat is very lightly tidied so that the dog has a neater outline, but still retains its natural look in the show ring. This breed, whose name is so descriptive, was not officially recognized until 1937 but has had a long history as a farming dog in the area of Ireland around Munster. They were required to do very much the same sort of work as the Kerry Blue did elsewhere in Ireland, though they are a slightly smaller and stockier animal, being 18in in height and about 40lb weight. The adult coat should be the shade of ripening wheat. The puppies are much darker and their hair lightens to the correct color as they mature.

Soft-coated Wheaten Terrier

The **Cairn Terrier** and the **West Highland White Terrier** share the same mixed ancestry. They both come from Scotland, the home of no less than five of the short-legged terrier breeds. None of these were clearly defined in either looks or type much before the beginning of this century. All were expected to do the same sort of work, helping to keep down the numbers of rats and mice. To do this effectively, they had to be small enough to go underground, agile enough to wriggle their way through crannies in piles of rocks, hardy enough to withstand the Scottish weather, and courageous enough to tackle anything from a rat to a polecat or fox.

The **West Highland White Terrier**, like many terriers, is a cheerful extrovert and has become very

**Cairn
Terrier**

CAIRN TERRIER / WEST HIGHLAND WHITE

West Highland White Terriers

popular, both as a show dog and a pet. All Westies have to have their coats stripped out twice a year, and preparing the coat of a show dog is now an art in itself. However, the correct double coat, with its harsh outer hair, is easy to keep clean, even though the color is always white. The hard, coarse jacket sheds dirt as easily as it sheds water.

The **Cairn Terrier** and the Westie are about the same size, 10in at the shoulder. The Cairn, however, presents a more shaggy and natural appearance. Coat colors include red, sandy, gray and brindled; dark ears and muzzle are very typical in the breed.

231

The **Scottish Terrier** was awarded its name in 1882, when agreement had at last been reached as to which among the welter of short-legged terriers in Scotland should merit the national name. The Scottish Terrier Club was formed the same year. In earlier days they were often called Aberdeen Terriers, which suggests the area that produced this particular type. They are the powerful heavyweight among the small terriers, being 23lb in weight and 11in in height. They are rather dour dogs, both independent and stubborn, having no time for outsiders but being very loyal to their owner and their home. The head of the Scottie is long, and trimmed so that the beard makes it appear even longer. Though black is the best known color both brindle and wheaten are equally correct. The coat needs stripping at least twice a year, and the show trim is complex.

Scottish Terrier

Sealyham Terriers

The **Sealyham Terrier** weighs about 20lb sand its height should not exceed 12in. The breed comes from Wales, where it was created during the second half of the 19th century by a sportsman who lived in Sealyham House in Pembrokeshire. It was developed to tackle badger and fox underground, and today they are still alert and fearless dogs. Their courage goes with a stubborn streak which makes early training advisable, but they should be friendly dogs and have a sense of fun which gives them a great deal of charm. The coat is profuse and needs regular attention to which the dog must become accustomed at an early age. The color is always white, but there can be lemon, brown, or black and white pied markings on the head and ears. Too much bathing softens the coat, which makes it get dirty more quickly and removes its weather resistant qualities.

The **Dandie Dinmont** is a terrier with a very distinctive outline. The body is long, strong, and flexible, with a curvaceous backline which gives the dog a weasel-like shape. The domed head is covered with a profuse, fine silky topknot which dramatically sets off the rich, dark hazel eyes. These round, lustrous eyes have a melting expression which rather belies the Dandie's character, for this a dog of great determination and strong individuality. They were renowned for the tenacity and courage when tackling otter, fox, and badger. Today's dog still retains the perseverance needed when battling with a foe larger than itself. The height should be about 22in and the body is longer than the dog is high by nearly two to one. The weight is about 23lb. Two colors are correct: either "pepper" (shades of gray) or "mustard" (shades of tan).

Dandy Dinmont Terrier

Skye Terrier

The **Skye Terrier** is now very much an exhibitor's dog, since the modern Skye has a floor-length coat which makes it rather an impracticable household pet. Skyes are very dramatic looking dogs, being very long and low to the ground. The height should be about 10in and the length 41½in, whilst the weight is 25lb. From these measurements it can be seen that the Skye is rather a hefty dog on rather short legs. The outer coat should be straight and hard in texture, hanging over a soft and woolly undercoat. The dog's face is veiled with hair and its long coat hangs down in a sweeping curtain completely obscuring the outline of the body. The long tail is gracefully feathered. Skyes can be any shade of gray, fawn, or cream but must always have a black nose and black ears.

235

Australian Terrier

The **Australian Terrier** is one of the few Terrier breeds developed outside the British Isles. Its history can only be traced for 100 years or so and its ancestors were a mixed bag of small terriers with very obvious Yorkshire Terrier influence. The desirable weight is 14lb and the height about 10in, so this is a very small working terrier. It is also a very active, agile, quick to pounce dog, with the hard and brilliant stare of a committed hunter of small game. It is reputed to have keen eye sight and quick reflexes and is supposed to be fast enough to kill the occasional snake in its homeland. It appears a rugged dog. The color can either be any shade of blue with rich tan markings, or it can be a clear sand on red.

The **Jack Russell Terrier** is a very popular pet. As type varies a great deal in the Jack Russell there will certainly be a lot of argument before a standard description is drawn up which suits all who are interested in this kind of terrier. Some adherents favor a long-legged type, which looks like early Fox Terriers, others favor dogs which are short and bowed in the leg like the Glen of Imaal Terrier. The color is predominantly white with patches of black or brown. Coats can be either smooth or rough and ear carriage is equally diverse.

Jack Russell Terrier

Index

239